From Pearl Harbor to V-J Day

FROM
PEARL HARBOR
TO V-J DAY

*The American Armed Forces
in World War II*

D. Clayton James
Anne Sharp Wells

The American Ways Series

IVAN R. DEE   *Chicago*

Maps by Victor Thompson, based on drawings by the authors

Library of Congress Cataloging-in-Publication Data:
James, D. Clayton.
    From Pearl Harbor to V-J Day : the American Armed Forces
in World War II / D. Clayton James, Anne Sharp Wells.
        p.   cm. — (The American ways series)
    Includes bibliographical references and index.
    ISBN 1-56663-072-X. — ISBN 1-56663-073-8 (pbk.)
    1. World War, 1939–1945—United States. 2. United States—
Armed Forces—History—World War, 1939–1945. I. Wells,
Anne Sharp. II. Title. III. Series.
D769.J36 1995
940.54'1273—dc20   94-24413

To the M. S. Worleys
and the N. E. Jameses

Contents

Maps

Foreword

THE SECOND WORLD WAR was history's largest war in numbers of nations and ground, sea, and air personnel. It was also the most expensive war in casualties, property destruction, and financial and economic costs. It was the first truly global war, consisting of active theaters of operations in the Atlantic, Western Europe, the Mediterranean, Eastern Europe, the Soviet Union, the Middle East, North Africa, Northwest Africa, China, India, Burma, Southeast Asia, and virtually all of the Pacific. Twenty-six Allied nations fought three Axis powers and their satellites.

Like the Confederates in the American Civil War, the Axis in World War II seemed doomed to defeat, possessing inferior manpower, economic resources, and firepower. Moreover, the Axis Pact was a frail alliance for Germany, Japan, and Italy, for their differences were so great that none was able to establish effective communications and cooperation with the other two. On the other hand, the United States and the United Kingdom forged a uniquely powerful "special relationship." Their gifted Combined Chiefs of Staff guided the strategic, command, and logistical activities of the Western Allies with superb leadership. Had the Axis coalition enjoyed such an effective alliance, the result might have been a protracted war, possibly resulting in a negotiated peace rather than unconditional surrender. The United States, which had been the junior member of the Allied Supreme War Council in World War I, now emerged as the mass producer of weaponry and the food supplier for all the Allies, as well as the relief provider for war-torn liberated countries.

The two nations that meshed into neither alliance but

maintained autonomous fronts against huge Axis forces were the Soviet Union and China, both of whom suffered the heaviest losses in lives and property of any nations in the war. American efforts to work with these distrustful (and, to a large extent, distrusted) opponents of the Axis were disappointing. Mutual feelings of suspicion and misunderstanding growing out of World War II would culminate in the momentous Chinese civil war and the East-West cold war. The postwar struggle of communism versus democracy was evolving even as the world of Axis totalitarianism was collapsing by 1943–1944.

This book examines the strategy, logistics, high command, operations, and home-front aspects of the American armed forces' involvement in this most complex and deadly of all wars. It is one of the most dramatic and significant periods of history, fraught with issues and crises that cast long shadows into the future. World War II was undoubtedly the most sublime and horrible of modern man's achievements.

The Virginia Military Institute provided invaluable assistance in many ways in helping us to prepare this book. Erlene James was indispensable in proofreading and timely counsel, as she has been on our previous books. Our thanks go also to Ivan Dee and John Braeman, our publisher and series editor, who provided excellent help in guiding the manuscript to publication.

D. Clayton James
Anne Sharp Wells

September 1994
Virginia Military Institute

From Pearl Harbor to V-J Day

PART ONE

Mobilizing and Planning

1

Ready or Not?

DURING THE SUMMER of 1941 in Louisiana the United States Army conducted the largest maneuvers in its history. For nearly two months the Second and Third armies collided in mock battle across bayous, swamps, fields, and hills, over soils that ranged from red clay to black loess, and in weather that varied from frequent thunderstorms to energy-draining heat. The maneuvers proved invaluable in testing weapons, training soldiers, and identifying commanders likely to succeed or fail in real action.

Assessments of the army's combat readiness differed greatly depending upon the viewer's perspective. The extremely able army chief of staff, General George C. Marshall, found much in the Louisiana performances to criticize and some aspects worth praise, such as the operational planning of Colonel Dwight D. "Ike" Eisenhower. Marshall's major concerns included a lack of coordination in moving large units in the field and in executing combined operations (infantry, artillery, armor, and aircraft).

On the other hand, the perspective of D. Clayton James was quite different. As a ten-year-old living in Natchez, Mississippi, he watched with wild-eyed fascination as thousands of troops and hundreds of military vehicles moved through the region, across the mighty Mississippi River, and into the bottomlands of Concordia Parish to the west. Often he and his young fellow adventurers sneaked across the bayou near his house to get closer looks at military trains temporarily stopped in the railyard. The sight of artillery, half-tracks, and light tanks on the flat cars, guarded by troops with machine guns, was awesome to the youngsters. But sometimes when fast-moving convoys drove through Natchez, the boys wondered why so many of the trucks looked old, why some of them bore cardboard signs saying "Heavy Tank," and why the soldiers in the trucks often carried wooden rifles.

In fact, the progress of America's armed services after the First World War had been slow and uneven. During the twenties and thirties isolationism and pacifism had gripped much of the public, while financial stringency and unimaginative, shortsighted leadership had plagued the defense establishment. With the onset of the Great Depression, both the Hoover and Roosevelt administrations focused on the unprecedented economic crisis instead of the aggressions of the fast-rising expansionist powers—Germany, Italy, and Japan. By the autumn of 1941 it was dubious whether America's combat readiness could match that of the principal belligerents of World War II, already two years under way in Europe and four years old in Asia. The crucial areas in doubt were military technology, tactical doctrine, economic and manpower mobilization, and strategic planning.

On paper the National Defense Act of 1920 had incorporated significant lessons military leaders had drawn from the Great War. But economy-minded, Republican-dominated Congresses during the 1920s refused to fund reforms called for by the legislation, notably tactical modernization and larger, better-trained peacetime regular and reserve forces. When the depressed thirties arrived, it was too late to boost military budgets enough to catch up with the world's other major powers. When General Douglas MacArthur was army chief of staff in 1933, the American army (including the army air corps) numbered only 135,000 troops, which placed it seventeenth in size among the world's armies, smaller even than Portugal's.

Because of the shortage of funds, especially for research and development, advances in army weaponry were not impressive between the world wars. Stockpiles of ordnance of 1917–1918 vintage became the pitiful legacy of the American soldier in the early days of World War II. The defense of the Philippines in 1941–1942, for instance, would be fought by American-Filipino troops with obsolete weapons and defective ammunition. The army had earlier developed a number of effective weapons, notably the Garand M-1 rifle (1936) and the 105 mm howitzer (1940), but they were not supplied in adequate numbers in time for the early campaigns.

Thanks to the efforts of Major George S. Patton, Jr., and other armor leaders, an American tank corps had fought in France in 1918. Afterward, however, tanks were considered only support weapons for the infantry while armor stalwarts vainly advocated their use as independent striking forces. By 1934 most of the leftover tanks from World War I, largely of French or British manufacture, were out of commission, and the army had only twelve post-1918 tanks in service. Several experimental mechanized forces were created under Major Adna R. Chaffee's leadership but received little funding and faced continuing hostility from infantry and cavalry leaders.

J. Walter Christie, an eccentric genius in tank design, developed promising tank models, but the War Department was apathetic toward his efforts. While the American army focused on light tanks in the thirties, the German and Soviet armies developed their Tiger and T-34 heavy tanks from Christie's designs. They moved ahead with innovative armored doctrine that made heavy and medium tanks essential to fast, powerful mechanized warfare.

After the German blitzkriegs in Poland and the Low Countries in 1939–1940—combined air and ground offensives of great speed and force—the War Department finally set up the Armored Force Command. Patton shortly thereafter was given command of the Desert Training Center in the Mojave Desert of California, where he and his fellow armor enthusiasts were able at last to obtain the resources to expedite the American effort.

This hasty but tardy progress in armor in the two years preceding U.S. entry into the war also included the development of the Sherman, a medium tank that became the workhorse of American armored forces despite numerous design flaws. Even in the crucial Normandy invasion in June 1944, American forces had to rely on Shermans to fight unequal duels against the much superior German Tigers and Panthers. In essence, the United States depended on its amazing ability in mass production to offset German quality in tank design. The long-touted legend of Yankee ingenuity was quietly supplanted by the reality of overwhelming numbers in armored firepower. The quantitative, rather than qualitative, edge applied to other weapons as well.

Army aviation was blessed with better support between the world wars by the War Department and Congress, due in part to the flying feats and crusades of army aeronautical pioneers. Most of them were ardent disciples of Brigadier General William Mitchell, who advocated an independent air force and the war-winning potential of strategic bombing. In the late 1930s the army air corps began to acquire growing numbers of two effective heavy bombers, the Boeing B-17 and the Consolidated B-24, whose performances further boosted American air leaders' beliefs in strategic air power. Unfortunately, they neglected the tactical and transport aspects of military aviation and entered World War II lacking fighters, medium bombers, transports, and other aircraft types that proved indispensable in supporting ground operations.

Since 1775 the American army had based its doctrines on the principles of firepower, mobility, and offensive action. The army's pre-1941 status does not suggest that its performances in the Second World War would reflect those principles. Fortunately, American industry's unprecedented output, the public's impressive support, and the timely appearance of a coterie of outstanding commanders all contributed to transform the nation's military forces into far more effective fighting arms than might have been anticipated.

After World War I the navy had enjoyed perhaps more success than the army in keeping pace with the forces of the world's other major powers. Even in this area, however, the United States had major weaknesses. The Washington and London naval limitation treaties of 1922 and 1930 had slowed the mounting naval arms race, led by Japan, but they had penalized the United States Navy especially by limitations on capital warships and base fortifications. The situation was aggravated by resistance to innovation from the "old guard" within the naval establishment.

American pioneers in carrier warfare were handicapped at the highest levels in the navy by powerful traditionalists who were heavily influenced by the thinking of Rear Admiral Alfred Thayer Mahan and his stress on climactic engagements by battleships. The disciples of Mahan saw carriers functioning mainly to protect battleships instead of operating independently as formidable strike forces against both surface naval units and land-based aircraft. But the *Lexington* and *Saratoga*, both commissioned in 1927, placed American carrier aviation and doctrine on a par with the Japanese and British navies. As with the advocates of armor, World War II vindicated those who had seen carriers as powerful offensive weapons systems.

The American navy's pioneers in submarine design and operations similarly faced obstruction by senior leaders who were dubious about the value of underseas warfare. A handful of determined submariners persisted in trying to develop an underseas fleet based on long-range submarines and reliable torpedoes. But they were limited by underfunding and bureaucratic hindrances, so America entered the Second World War seriously lagging in torpedo and submarine design and production compared with the other leading naval powers. As with other backward areas of American military technology in 1941, submarine and torpedo quality and quantity improved dramatically, and by 1945 American submarines sank more Japanese naval and merchant ships than were destroyed by both surface ships and aircraft.

Some of the navy's most important advances during the interwar period were led by the two most influential admirals in the coming conflict with Japan, Ernest J. King and Chester W. Nimitz. They devised an at-sea resupply system that allowed the Pacific Fleet to cruise for at least four months at a time without withdrawing to naval bases in Hawaii or California. Support vessels would accompany the Pacific Fleet's combat ships and permit them to remain on distant open-sea stations by providing fuel, munitions, repairs, and various supplies. This gave the American navy a staying capacity that the Japanese Combined Fleet lacked in lengthy operations.

The Marine Corps, meanwhile, was engaged in farsighted experiments in amphibious warfare. Where the British amphibious assault at Gallipoli in 1915 had dampened enthusiasm for this dimension of warfare, some American marine leaders saw it as a new justification for the marines if a war with Japan eventually erupted and involved chiefly naval battles and island assaults. As early as 1923, marine Major Earl H. Ellis became a fervent advocate of Marine Corps leadership in experimenting with amphibious attacks, especially considering a future clash with Japan. Ten years later Major General John H. Russell was named head of the newly created Fleet Marine Force, set up to specialize in amphibious warfare. In 1934 Russell's staff produced the *Tentative Manual of Landing Operations*, which also became the basic doctrinal guide for amphibious operations by the American army in World War II.

The marines' move into this complicated new realm of war gave the United States an important lead that it retained throughout World War II and afterward. The efforts of the Marine Corps were greatly aided by the work of Andrew Higgins, an enlightened shipbuilder in New Orleans and a firm believer in the marines' new mission. Higgins developed a number of experimental landing craft, beginning with the LCVP (Landing Craft, Vehicles and Personnel) in 1934. Much later he and other ship designers created sea-going assault vessels, the most significant being the LST (Landing Ship, Tanks). Among those who learned to appreciate the various types of landing vessels was British Prime Minister Winston Churchill, who later maintained that, more than any other weapon of World War II, their adequate numbers determined which Anglo-American seaborne assaults could be conducted.

A 1930s technological breakthrough that vitally affected America's military and diplomatic capabilities in the approaching war was the brilliant achievement of code-breakers in the War Department, led by William F. Friedman. This was Magic, a system of decrypting high-level Japanese diplomatic messages. Also before the war, American cryptanalysts had made progress on Japanese army and navy codes, though the main intercepts of such radio intelligence (later called Ultra-J) would come after the beginning of hostilities between the U.S. and Japan. Luckily, during the prewar era the Japanese had no inkling that its key diplomatic and military codes were vulnerable.

If American military accomplishments in technology and doctrine were of mixed quality before 1941, this was even more true of planning in the War and Navy departments on economic and manpower mobilization and on strategy. A commendable start was the inclusion in the National Defense Act of 1920 of the new position of assistant secretary of war for procurement, who would be responsible for the army's peacetime planning for future manpower and material needs. Also, the navy was charged with responsibility for its mobilization planning. For the next two decades, generals and admirals in Washington made well-intended, if often ineffective, attempts to achieve peacetime coordination between war-related industries and the military.

In 1922 the Joint Army-Navy Munitions Board was established as the military's basic planning agency in weapons systems and ordnance used by both services. The following

year the Army Industrial College was set up in Washington
to educate selected officers of both services in matters of
wartime industrial problems. A notable advance was the
Industrial Mobilization Plan of 1933, a farsighted initiative based on study by army Chief of Staff MacArthur's
office, and led by Major Dwight Eisenhower; and President
Hoover's earlier War Policies Commission, headed by financier Bernard Baruch. More planning in the thirties focused
on strategic raw materials and manufactures that the military would need in a national emergency. Also carefully
considered were priorities and allocations that were likely to
be troublesome, based on World War I experience.

These military and civilian planners tried to anticipate the
many federal agencies that would be required for economic
mobilization in case of war. The planners could not foresee
that President Franklin D. Roosevelt would largely ignore
their considerable investment in improving and implementing the 1933 plan.

Besides mobilization of the economy in time of war,
manpower planning was crucial. When General Malin Craig
succeeded MacArthur as army chief of staff in 1935, he
accelerated work in this field. Two years later the Pro-
tective Mobilization Plan provided for 400,000 regular army
troops and National Guardsmen as an initial force at the
outbreak of hostilities and a gradual expansion of the army
to four million men. In the summer of 1941, Brigadier
General Albert C. Wedemeyer delivered to Chief of Staff
Marshall the well-conceived Victory Plan. It projected with
uncanny accuracy the army's personnel needs for World War
II. Considering the anticipated heavy responsibility of the
United States to provide food, relief, and military equipment
for its allies, Wedemeyer predicted that American manpower
commitments for agricultural and manufacturing production would leave the army with a basic reservoir of about
eight million young men from which to draw.

The often-repeated assertion that American armed forces
were unprepared when Japan attacked Hawaii in December

1941 is untrue in terms of personnel growth. When Hitler's panzers rolled into Poland in September 1939, the United States Army (including the army air corps) had 190,000 men and officers; the navy numbered 125,000 and the marines 19,000; the services' grand total was 334,000. The growth in the next two years shows movement toward preparedness: by the time of Japan's Pearl Harbor attack in 1941, the personnel strength of the American services totaled 1.8 million, with 1.5 million in the army, 284,000 in the navy, and 54,000 in the Marine Corps. By the end of the war against Japan in 1945, the grand total was 12.1 million, the army (including the army air forces) having grown to 8.3 million, the navy to 3.4 million, and the marines to 475,000.

American military planners had long anticipated future strategic as well as mobilization needs and problems. Even before World War I, the War and Navy departments had begun work on a series of "color plans," wherein a color designated the strategic plan to be implemented if a certain country went to war against the United States. From the early 1920s onward, War Plan Orange, denoting a possible conflict with Japan, received the most attention. Several editions of Orange culminated in 1938 in WPO-3, which was in effect when the Pearl Harbor raid occurred in late 1941.

The background of WPO-3 involved complicated, repetitive, and tense debates between army and navy planners. By the early 1930s both services foresaw any American-Japanese war as costly and lengthy, with an early Japanese capture of the Philippines, an American territory since 1898. The navy had long favored a Central Pacific counteroffensive, led by navy and marine forces, to seize the Japanese-mandated Mariana, Marshall, and Caroline islands. American reaction to Japanese aggression would secure the line of communications from Hawaii to the Philippines, thus paving the way for the reinforcement or reconquest of that American archipelago.

Army planners maintained that American strength in the

Philippines, which consisted of the antiquated Asiatic Fleet and the tiny Philippine Department of the United States Army, would not be able to stop a sizable Japanese invasion force. Army spokesmen argued that Filipino and American defenders would be defeated before reinforcements could arrive from Hawaii, particularly in view of likely Japanese supremacy in the skies and seas of the Philippines. While the army recommended the transfer of all American forces from the archipelago, navy planners saw a major role for their ships in the West Pacific and therefore opposed a withdrawal from the Philippines.

In WPO-3 the two services reached a compromise of sorts. The navy managed to delete from the plan an army-favored clause that required presidential approval of naval offensives west of Hawaii. In turn, the army succeeded in striking references to an early navy-marine advance across the West Pacific. WPO-3 stipulated that American and Filipino forces were to defend the mouth of Manila Bay. But it failed to specify how long the navy would take to reach the islands and gave little encouragement about the relief of the defenders. If the army and navy had not solved the dilemma of the islands' security, the American Congress had demonstrated between the world wars that it was also ambivalent, providing neither adequate funds for Philippine defenses nor authorization for American forces to withdraw.

By the beginning of war in Europe in 1939, American army and navy planners in Washington had come to realize that the color plans were unrealistic in preparing for American belligerency against a single enemy. They shifted to five plans in a rainbow series, setting up hypothetical war scenarios involving various alliances on each side and multiple theaters of operations. Rainbow-5 was the plan that most accurately approximated the Axis and Allied coalitions and zones of combat that developed in World War II. It assumed the Philippines' early capitulation and strategic defensive efforts against Japan's offensive until Anglo-American forces could be redeployed from Europe after the surrender of Germany and Italy.

Admiral Harold R. Stark, chief of naval operations, produced a corollary study in November 1940, the Plan Dog Memorandum, which argued against an American priority for a Pacific war if Germany and Japan were the opposing belligerents. It favored concerted Anglo-American operations until victory was first gained against the European Axis. From January to March 1941, secret talks in Washington between high-level American and British officers resulted in the ABC-1 Report. It unequivocally set forth the two fundamental principles that would guide American and British general strategy throughout World War II. First, if the United States came into the conflict, it would enter into a firm and special alliance with the United Kingdom involving close cooperation in logistics, strategy, and operations. Second, the Anglo-American alliance would commit itself to the defeat of Germany first, since that nation was the most powerful and dangerous member of the Axis coalition.

2

The Military and the Home Front

THE UNITED STATES formally entered the war against Japan on December 8, 1941, one day after the surprise Japanese attack on American bases at Pearl Harbor and elsewhere on the island of Oahu in Hawaii. Three days later the governments of Germany and Italy, in support of their Axis Pact ally, declared war against the United States. Although American preparedness for war had already begun with the expansion of the armed forces and the defense industry, the country reacted with shock and anger at the onset of real war. Isolationist movements died quickly as most of the public united behind the war effort.

In the immediate aftermath of the raid on Hawaii, many Americans feared that the Axis powers would bomb or invade the United States. Sabotage was another acute concern. The military was placed on full alert, with guards assigned to government buildings, bases, defense factories, bridges, and other vital sites. Guns were installed on the roofs of important buildings such as the White House. Blackouts were imposed throughout the country, although enforcement was haphazard in some areas. Not only civilian residents but military and naval forces on the West Coast overreacted to alarmist reports of imminent attacks or invasions by Japanese armadas approaching the United States. The most extreme example of fear and anger was the internment of some 112,000 people of Japanese ancestry, many of them American citizens, who were forced to leave their homes, losing property and businesses in the process, and move to barren camps set up in isolated locations across the country. The evacuation was authorized by Executive Order 9066 on February 16, 1942, and was supervised by army troops under Lieutenant General John L. DeWitt, head of the West Coast Defense Command. Believing that the loyalty of the Japanese-Americans was suspect, DeWitt had recommended that they be relocated in order to prevent spying and sabotage in "military zones" in the western United States. Ironically, while Japanese-Americans on the West Coast were placed in concentration camps, Japanese-Americans from Hawaii entered the army and gained distinction in combat. More than 5,000 Americans of German and Italian ancestry were also interned at the beginning of the war, but most were released within a year.

When war began, the draft was already in place, with the Selective Service system authorized in September 1940 and extended the following year (by one vote in Congress). Originally, men between the ages of twenty-one and thirty-five were required to register with local officials; the limits were later extended to include ages from eighteen to sixty-four, although the highest age actually conscripted was thirty-eight. Draftees comprised ten million of the sixteen million members of the armed forces in 1941–1945. Approximately one-sixth of American males served in the military during the war. Deferments were granted for certain agricultural and industrial occupations that the government deemed vital for the war effort. Most of the men who were rejected (6.4 million) "had medical defects that would not have spared them from service in other countries," says a reliable source, adding: "The draft officers found only 510,000 registrants absolutely disqualified for service."

The regular armed forces were augmented by women who volunteered for service. In 1942 Congress, responding to projections of manpower shortages, authorized the Women's Auxiliary Army Corps, later shortened to Women's

Army Corps (WAC). Also formed were the navy's Women Accepted for Volunteer Emergency Services (WAVES), the Coast Guard's SPARs, and an unnamed force of women in the marines. The most prominent spokesperson for women in the military was the director of the WACs, Colonel Oveta Culp Hobby, a former newspaper editor from Houston, Texas, who had also worked in public relations for the War Department. Women were given noncombatant military jobs with the idea that more men would then be released for combat slots. At first, women in the services were assigned chiefly to stateside jobs as clerical workers, telephone operators, and motor pool drivers, but as the war progressed they performed a wide variety of tasks, both in the States and overseas, serving as cryptographers, radio operators, mechanics, photographers, laboratory technicians, translators, and pilots for ferrying planes.

Industrial mobilization began with numerous hitches and mistakes, but it gained momentum far more quickly than in the First World War. It reached a peak in 1944, when the production of war materials began to be cut back. Current production was then considered adequate to meet U.S. and Allied needs to the end of hostilities. Too, economists and manufacturers favored a precautionary downsizing of the red-hot industrial machinery to avert a painful economic dislocation, especially job layoffs, similar to the one that had followed World War I and precipitated the sharp recession of 1919–1922.

The huge acceleration of industrial output was centered in the automotive world, which had long led the way in mass production. Detroit's conversion from Fords and Chevrolets to Sherman tanks and other military vehicles was made easier by the use of existing factory equipment that needed modification but not necessarily replacement. Outstanding was Ford's enormous Willow Run, Michigan, plant of more than nine hundred acres under one roof; Willow Run workers, thanks to ingenious changes in the long assembly lines, adapted to building first tanks, then B-24 heavy bombers (more than fifty thousand), parts of ships, and other instruments of war. Mass-production facilities elsewhere around the country were modified rapidly to handle conversions from peacetime manufactures to weapons and other military equipment. In 1944 aircraft production in the United States reached the amazing annual total of 96,300; in contrast, that year Germany also achieved its highest yearly figure, 40,600, while Japan's 1944 total was only 28,000. During the years 1941–1945, American tank production totaled 61,000, compared with 20,000 for Germany and 2,500 for Japan.

Beyond the great U.S. prewar lead in industrialization, its pioneering efforts in mass production, and the success of the automotive companies in wartime conversion, the "Arsenal of Democracy" became a reality also because of gifted, imaginative, and energetic captains of industry. Like the Marshalls and Eisenhowers of the military realm, they rose to meet the challenges of the national emergency. Many entrepreneurs could be cited, but surely the two outstanding ones were Andrew J. Higgins and Henry J. Kaiser.

Higgins has been described as "a hard-drinking, tough-talking swamp rat and boat genius" who established gigantic shipyard facilities in New Orleans employing more than thirty thousand workers. His name became synonymous with the fledgling landing-craft program, also under way in other yards on a smaller scale. Altogether, more than twenty thousand Higgins boats were used by the navy, including fifteen hundred craft at Omaha and Utah beaches in Normandy on D-day, June 6, 1944. Most of his boats were LCIs (Landing Craft, Infantry) and LCVPs, which, unlike the seagoing LSTs, were carried aboard transport ships to amphibious assault sites from the Mediterranean and the English Channel to the Pacific islands. The marines were especially grateful to Higgins for encouraging their research and development of amphibious warfare doctrine and equipment before and during the Second World War.

Kaiser was a hard-driving, supremely self-confident, imaginative entrepreneur in the mold of the giants of late-nineteenth-century industry. Before the war his companies were involved in highway construction, the building of great dams, and cement and steel manufacturing. He was famous too for his innovations in prefabrication and novel construction methods. Although his wartime efforts spanned a number of types of war materiel production, his most significant contribution was in building the great fleet of "Liberty Ships." His facilities could turn out one of these 10,500-ton freighters in less than a week. He built other cargo ships too, and by the end of the war had constructed about a third of the entire U.S. merchant marine. As top commanders and logisticians during the war knew, landing craft and shipping were probably the most critical needs the armed forces had in determining successful operations. Higgins and Kaiser could not have hit their strides at a more opportune time. Their roles in World War II construction were comparable to the contribution by Robert Morris as "the financier of the American Revolution."

Leaders of big business could not have achieved their war production goals without the commitment of labor, both trade unions and unorganized workers. Pay, especially overtime, and benefits were generous, and the war meant the end of the unemployment lines of the Great Depression that had gripped the country since 1929. Millions of American families were on the move during the war years, with California's large concentration of defense industries luring most of them. Almost overnight, factories making war materials were desperate for workers, so that they could fulfill profitable contracts for orders placed by the War and Navy departments. The demographic shifts were usually to large urban centers with innumerable job openings in defense plants and excellent opportunities for civilian employment on nearby military and naval installations. The urban trend caused farm population to decline 17 percent from 1941 to 1945, though better farming practices and more intensive cultivation led to record crops, the surpluses going mainly to Allied countries.

Organized labor in effect negotiated with the federal government and big business a no-strike pledge for the duration of the war, and it was largely honored. Several new federal agencies helped oversee the wartime labor-management truce, notably the National War Labor Board and the National Defense Mediation Board. The main violators were the aggressive John L. Lewis and his United Mine Workers, who staged several crippling strikes that in 1943 led to the U.S. government's seizure of the mines, threats to draft strikers, and passage of the War Labor Disputes Act to better control such problems.

An important group mobilized for defense purposes was the scientific community, whose efforts were coordinated by the Office of Scientific Research and Development (OSRD), headed by Dr. Vannevar Bush. Advising the OSRD were the National Defense Research Committee and the Committee on Medical Research. A great deal of war-related research was carried out in the laboratories of universities and industries, working under government contracts. In addition to making new discoveries, scientists in the United States developed and improved inventions that had originated in other countries. Among their significant contributions to the war effort were radar, sonar, radio proximity fuses, antitank rockets, and jet aircraft.

The most dramatic scientific development was the atomic bomb. During the first part of the war atomic research was coordinated by the OSRD and the army, but in 1943 the Manhattan District of the U.S. Army Corps of Engineers was set up to direct the development of atomic weapons. Major General Leslie R. Groves assumed command of the "Manhattan Project"; he reported directly to Secretary of War Henry L. Stimson and army Chief of Staff Marshall. Much of the work was based in three locations: Oak Ridge, Tennessee; Hanford, Washington; and Los Alamos, New Mexico. The bomb was built in Los Alamos under the direction of physicist J. Robert Oppenheimer. The entire project was carried out under highly secretive conditions; even its funding was hidden within the army budget throughout much of the war.

Advancements in medicine contributed significantly to the lives of American servicemen, who faced a variety of diseases and hostile climates as well as combat injuries. Penicillin, which had been discovered earlier in Europe, was developed, mass produced, and distributed by the United States during the war. It was first used by the military in the spring of 1943. Sulfa drugs, first used in the 1930s, made another vital contribution to saving lives. A typhus vaccine was developed and successfully tested, while DDT was used to control disease-spreading lice. Antihistamines also were discovered, beginning with Benadryl in 1943. Antimalarial programs included the prescription of the drug Atabrine, the use of DDT to kill mosquitoes, and the activation of special military units to control the spread of the disease. Research into the treatment of injured soldiers with whole blood instead of plasma led to the creation of blood banks, the shipment of whole blood overseas, and new transfusion methods.

Blacks and other minorities, as well as women, were strongly affected by the changed economic circumstances of wartime. They were accepted into defense jobs in large numbers, though grudgingly at first by some companies. President Roosevelt's establishment of the Fair Employment Practices Commission helped somewhat to curb racial and gender prejudice, but the pay received by African Americans and women—though showing improvement—lagged behind that of white males in similar positions.

The already overcrowded black ghettos in Northern cities, especially in Chicago and Detroit, became even more congested with mass arrivals of families from the rural South. Racial conflict exploded in several cities, triggered by tensions over lack of adequate housing, alleged unfair and disproportionately high drafting of blacks for the military, and police brutality, particularly in the mistreatment of returning black servicemen. The Detroit race riot of June 1943 left 25 blacks and 9 whites dead, 675 people injured, and $2 million in property destroyed. A rumor of a black soldier's killing by a policeman was the immediate cause of a riot in Harlem that August, resulting in 6 blacks dead, 400 injured, and property damage of $5 million.

Latinos too enjoyed opportunities in defense work and the military but faced discrimination and the lack of a political voice and economic power. Latino frustrations also erupted primarily in large cities, especially in Los Angeles. In a riot there in June 1943, white sailors and Latinos brawled over women and then rampaged through a large area, looting and destroying property.

Native Americans, fifty thousand strong, also worked in defense industries while others served in the armed services. The Navajos' service as code talkers for the marines during the battle for Iwo Jima was the most unique minority contribution to the combat arena. Comparatively small in numbers and isolated largely on reservations with few work possibilities, most of the Native Americans who left to enter the military or the defense work force returned home at the end of the war, having found assimilation into the domain of the white male as difficult as it was for blacks and Latinos.

As the war neared its end, it was not uncommon for defense industries to lay off all or most of its workers who were women or members of minorities. The war period had seemed at first like the threshold of a new age for all these groups, but the image of an imminent utopia disappeared with these clearly biased layoffs as the war effort wound down.

The rise of hundreds of training camps, airfields, and naval installations across the land shook the urban suburbs and small towns of America. The boys overseas may have been heroes to the local populace, but when based nearby they were often ostracized or regarded as troublemakers interested only in drinking, gambling, fighting, or chasing women. Brawls between local men and troops were frequent in bars, restaurants, and other public areas when servicemen came to town on weekend passes. Civilians also groused about the long convoys that tied up highways and caused lengthy traffic jams, passing through towns whose narrow streets were ill equipped for thousands of fast-moving military vehicles. On trains and buses, civilians and troops were often less than gracious toward each other when a military group boarded and created a crowded situation, sometimes exacerbated by drinking on both sides. Fortunately, most large military personnel transfers were made on trains reserved for that purpose, though public discontent often was heard over the decline of passenger trains.

One of the strange rituals born during the war was the hazardous low-level "buzzing" of hometowns by local boys who had become military or naval pilots. These bizarre episodes were viewed as good for the morale of both the residents and the pilots, though too many times they ended in flaming crashes. A more sane celebration was the periodic town turnout for a decorated hero who had been sent by the Pentagon on a tour to promote war-bond sales. All kinds of drives, whether for scrap metal, rubber, paper, or bonds, were inevitably huge successes, so enthusiastic were most small-town citizens and so pressured socially were most of the rest.

Prison camps also dotted the American landscape. German and Italian captives were comparatively well treated in prisoner-of-war camps in the United States. As with any groups of considerable size, some Axis troops returned home after the war with memories of injustices, but they were perpetrated by individuals and not supported by U.S. policy and officials governing the POW camp system in the States. In a number of cases, Axis prisoners were permitted to leave the camps both for leisure time and to participate in local events of nearby towns, ranging from festivals to crop harvests.

The total number of prisoners held by the Allies (except for those in the USSR, which is unknown) was 1.1 million, of which 425,000 were in camps in the United States. Two-thirds of the 511 prison camps in America were in the South and Southwest, with 120 in Texas—the most of any state. One source suggests that Texas may have been used "because POWs had nowhere to hide if they tried to escape." An unexpected number of the Germans were cooperative and appeared happy to be out of harm's way. At war's end, some POWs resisted their return to homelands ravaged by war and preferred to stay in America.

Not only were captured Axis troops treated better than might be expected, but returning American servicemen received federal assistance far beyond any veterans' aid that had been provided in United States history. Although President Roosevelt had announced in December 1943 that "Dr. New Deal" had been replaced by "Dr. Win the War," he referred in his State of the Union message the next month to the need for an "economic bill of rights" for the American people, and that spring he strongly endorsed the Servicemen's Readjustment Bill. This measure, though falling short of the social engineering goals that New Dealers envisioned, bestowed such widespread veterans' benefits that it had enormous economic and social impact in the postwar era.

The legislation won bipartisan support and was signed into law by FDR in June 1944. By then more than a million GIs had returned home, many wounded or handicapped. The "GI Bill of Rights," as the act became known, was a great help to many of them and to millions more who served in World War II. Its multifaceted aid programs included a year's worth of generous unemployment compensation to veterans unable to find jobs, and funding for veterans to buy houses, farms, or small businesses. The bill even covered burial expenses. It profoundly boosted the home-building industry and helped to change the majority of American families from renters to home-owners. One of every five new single-family houses built between 1944 and 1966 was financed by the GI Bill. Its provisions for physical and psychological rehabilitation were substantial, including large numbers of new Veterans Administration hospitals and services for the wounded in spirit and body.

The GI Bill gave free tuition, subsistence, and books to returning servicemen who undertook a college education or vocational training. Nearly eight million GIs were enabled to attend college or vocational schools, and more than $14 billion was paid out for higher education and job training. The bill helped to trigger a remarkable postwar era of growth in higher education. Duke University, for instance, had to launch a rapid building program to cope with an enrollment that doubled between 1945 and 1948. By 1947 half of all college students in the United States were veterans. Faculty members and nonveteran students faced major adjustments, as did the ex-GIs, when this unique influx of older and war-toughened young men, who had been forced to lose their youth, came to campus. More responsible than the other students, the veterans generally excelled in the classroom, in sports, and in courting college women.

The GI Bill may have been the last hurrah of the virtually moribund New Deal, but in countless ways it changed the outlook and opportunities of a generation of postwar American young adults. Many of the nation's future leaders in politics, business, education, and other fields were beneficiaries of the Servicemen's Readjustment Act, arguably the most significant of all reforms in the FDR era.

3

The Top Levels

THE ANGLO-AMERICAN ALLIANCE attained marked superiority over the Axis powers in four key dimensions: high command, strategy, logistics, and intelligence. From late 1943 onward the United States dominated the Western coalition and these areas, in contrast to its secondary impact at the top levels during World War I. Of the other twenty-four nations on the Allied side, the main contributors to victory were the Soviet Union, China, France, and Australia, but they often felt like unequal partners. Rarely did the United States and the United Kingdom allow them full access to their plans and resources.

During the four decades before American entry into World War II, United States policy toward Asia had been rather interventionist in its economic and moralistic diplomacy, while its policy toward Europe had been largely passive or cautious. In the years 1941 to 1945, however, the principal U.S. goals in the Pacific conflict were to defeat Japan; to keep China fighting, especially the Nationalists; to reopen American access to strategic resources in Asia, particularly oil, rubber, and bauxite; and to dominate direction of Allied military operations and postwar planning regarding Japan and the West Pacific.

In Europe, the foremost American objectives were to bring about the capitulation of Nazi Germany and fascist Italy, preferably through a war of massive confrontation rather than protracted attrition; to coordinate military efforts with Great Britain as closely as necessary to ensure the survival of their special relationship and indeed of Western civilization; and to support the Soviet Union with substantial shipments of aid and with diplomatic overtures toward closer relations. While Roosevelt, Churchill, and Stalin negotiated the political and economic shape of the postwar world, U.S. officials devoted little attention to postwar economic matters in European nations or in their colonies. From Washington to the American headquarters in Europe, the wartime focus was on military objectives.

America's contribution to the direction of the Allied war efforts was limited primarily to the Pacific, the Atlantic, Northwest Europe, Northwest Africa, Sicily, Italy, and Burma. In the theaters with the largest combat forces and the highest military and civilian casualties—the Soviet and Chinese fronts—America's strategic impact was negligible, though its Lend-Lease shipments of military and relief assistance were considerable. Marshal Joseph Stalin personally controlled the movement of his Soviet armies along the two-thousand-mile Eastern Front and brooked no interference from Western leaders, even when his troops penetrated deeply into Central Europe. Generalissimo Chiang Kai-shek similarly went his own way in overseeing his two fronts—against the Japanese and against the Chinese Communists.

In the spring of 1942 the newly formed Combined Chiefs of Staff, which mainly comprised the American and British service chiefs, delegated the strategic direction of the war in the Pacific to the American chiefs and in South Asia and the Indian Ocean to the British chiefs. The Combined Chiefs reserved to themselves the West European and Mediterranean theaters, as well as the Atlantic. The American chiefs proceeded quickly to establish two Pacific theaters: Pacific Ocean Areas, under Admiral Chester W. Nimitz, and the Southwest Pacific Area, under General Douglas MacArthur. In MacArthur's sphere, Australia proved to be an unexpected bonus, calling home her veteran divisions and air

units from the desert war in North Africa and contribut-
ing huge quantities of supplies and numbers of troops
for MacArthur's operations. Nevertheless, MacArthur and
Nimitz, with the endorsement of the American Joint Chiefs,
seldom sought strategic advice from the twelve lesser Allied
powers engaged in the war against Japan. Not until the
spring of 1945 did Britain succeed in deploying its Royal
Navy in Pacific operations.

The commander-in-chief of the American military establishment was President Roosevelt, not only by authority of
the Constitution but also by his liberal interpretation of his
war powers and his numerous interventions in military
affairs. By virtue of his experience as assistant secretary of
the navy in World War I and his lifelong love of sailing,
FDR was especially meddlesome in naval matters. He had a
formidable challenger in Churchill, who also considered
himself a first-rate naval authority, having served twice earlier
as first lord of the admiralty. In messages to the American
president, he anointed himself as "Former Naval Person."

In the shadows behind many a great leader has stood a
mysterious figure who has been his trusted confidant and
gifted adviser. Roosevelt was lucky in that respect, having
the calm and wise Harry L. Hopkins, who possessed a rare
perceptiveness regarding many key leaders and the uses of
force in diplomacy. He became the president's indispensable
liaison with Churchill and Stalin as well as with the American Joint Chiefs of Staff and the Anglo-American Combined
Chiefs of Staff. Churchill accurately described him as "Lord
Root of the Matter."

The next level of war direction below civilian control was
twofold—the United States Joint Chiefs of Staff and the
British-American Combined Chiefs of Staff. The American
JCS consisted of the principal ground, air, and sea commanders and a chairman who also functioned as chief of staff to
the president. The Combined Chiefs of Staff, established in
early 1942 like the Joint Chiefs, included the American
chiefs and their counterparts, called the British Chiefs of

Staff Committee. The American and British chiefs met together only at summit conferences, such as those at Casablanca, Quebec, Tehran, and Yalta, which were led by the American president and commander-in-chief, Roosevelt, and the British prime minister and defense minister, Churchill. Between these eleven major conferences, the Combined Chiefs communicated by cable and telephone almost daily. Important to the smooth functioning of their unique arrangement, both the American and British chiefs relied heavily on the large British Joint Staff Mission in Washington (more than three thousand personnel) to relay and explain positions of one side to the other.

The British mission was headed by a tactful, articulate former head of the British army, Field Marshal John Dill. He and General Marshall, the American army chief of staff, became devoted friends and communicated superbly with each other on critical issues. Their deep friendship was a blessing to the American alliance with Britain, comparable only to the close bond that developed between Roosevelt and Churchill. The importance of these two personal relationships is impossible to exaggerate in holding together the Anglo-American coalition at the top levels.

The chairman of the U.S. Joint Chiefs of Staff was Admiral William D. Leahy, a former chief of naval operations and a close friend of FDR. Coolheaded and usually formal, Leahy was widely respected in the navy, but his value to the president lay in his ability to communicate to the Joint Chiefs the president's thinking on various military issues and his prescience about future differences between the Western Allies and the Soviet Union. Long before most American leaders came to mistrust Stalin, Leahy sensed that his primary motivation was global Communist expansion. Leahy chaired the Joint Chiefs' meetings and alternated with British General Alan F. Brooke in heading the sessions of the Combined Chiefs.

Among American senior officers, General George C. Marshall commanded the most respect and influence, not only among his colleagues on the Joint Chiefs of Staff but also with British leaders. Churchill called him "a tower of strength and sagacity." He was admired for his professionalism, decisiveness, integrity, organizational ability, selection of leaders, comprehension of global strategy and logistics, and dignity and calm under stress. His flaws included a fiery temper, limited understanding of nonmilitary strategy, aloofness, and awesomeness to the point of intimidation. Marshall became the foremost proponent of an early invasion of Normandy.

Admiral Ernest J. King was the only American naval officer ever to hold simultaneously the positions of chief of naval operations and commander-in-chief of the United States Fleet. He was a volatile advocate of greater attention to the Pacific war, clashing on this issue with both Marshall and the British chiefs. He also strongly supported Admiral Nimitz's plans for a Central Pacific offensive over MacArthur's strategy for a Southwest Pacific advance. King's assets included his sharp intellect, forthrightness, determination, and versatile leadership in naval air, surface, and submarine planning and operations. On the other hand, he could be cruel and abrasive. Eisenhower called him "a mental bully," while British Admiral Andrew B. Cunningham found him to be "ill-mannered, ruthless, and arrogant." At the Cairo Conference in November 1943, King had to be restrained as he tried to crawl across the table to punch British General Brooke.

The fourth and final member of the American chiefs was General Henry H. "Hap" Arnold, commanding general of the army air forces. His major contributions at Joint and Combined Chiefs meetings concerned air warfare. He also fervently championed the Germany-first principle, the cross-channel assault on France, and all-out strategic bombing campaigns against Germany and Japan. Arnold was a pioneer of military aviation and became an imaginative experimenter with new technology in air warfare. He was dedicated to his job and earned the respect and affection of his colleagues. Among his liabilities were impatience, impetuosity, poor organizational skills, and, as one friend phrased it, his tendency to be "an incurable maverick." He also suffered from poor health, enduring four coronary attacks during the war.

Both the American and British chiefs relied on joint (or interservice) committees for the research and initial drafting of strategic and operational proposals to Churchill and Roosevelt. This committee system was also essential in handling the advance planning and preparation of directives to theater commanders. In the latter sense, Marshall and King acted as the executive agents for the Joint Chiefs in relations with MacArthur and Nimitz. The most important of the committees advising the Joint Chiefs was the Joint Staff Planners, which comprised some of the best and brightest senior army and navy staff officers. Among more than a dozen other committees, the most important were those dealing with war plans and logistics. They had their counterparts in the committee system of the British Chiefs of Staff. In turn, the Anglo-American chiefs set up the Combined Staff Planners, Combined War Plans Committee, and others paralleling the two national committee structures.

Toward the end of the war American strategic planning was slowed by this complex administrative apparatus, especially in the Combined Staff committees. Even in the Pacific, supposedly an American strategic domain, the senior commanders sometimes complained that the Joint Staff channels delayed crucial changes in operations necessitated by rapidly developing combat circumstances. It was not unusual for officers at theater headquarters to disparage the "committeeitis" that sometimes seemed to handicap the Joint and Combined Chiefs. From the theater perspective, it is no wonder that Washington and London seemed to be "running the war by committees."

Compromises characterized the evolution of Anglo-American strategy. Early in 1941 the British thought they had wrung from the Americans a firm pledge to a Germany-first priority. But because of the wrath of the American public over the attack on Pearl Harbor and atrocities such as the Bataan Death March, together with the surprising conquests by Japan in the Pacific, the United States was forced to send a majority of its overseas forces to the Pacific during the first two years of the war.

Another vital compromise involved the cross-channel assault on France. Churchill and his chiefs, knowing the potency of the German war machine and the shrinking reservoir of British manpower, preferred to postpone the Normandy invasion until Germany had been greatly weakened by strategic air bombardment and peripheral ground operations in North Africa and southern Europe. The Americans, with Marshall in the forefront, wanted to launch the ground attack through Normandy as soon as an adequate buildup of Allied forces in Britain could be achieved. Marshall even pushed for a limited cross-channel operation to begin in the autumn of 1942 if Germany or the Soviet Union appeared to be collapsing.

In a sense, the often stressful Anglo-American debate was between two extreme styles of war—attrition and an indirect strategy in the Mediterranean versus annihilation and direct confrontation in Northwest Europe. The British views prevailed largely during the summit conferences at Casablanca in January 1943 and at Washington in June 1942 and May 1943. Churchill won over FDR, and the two heads of state, together with the British Chiefs of Staff, persuaded the reluctant American Joint Chiefs to undertake the invasions of Northwest Africa, Sicily, and Italy between November 1942 and September 1943. These Mediterranean detours, as the American chiefs viewed them, killed a tentative agreement on the Normandy assault for May 1943. Postwar assessments generally concluded that landing in Normandy would have been disastrous in 1942 and probably so even in 1943.

A third major Anglo-American compromise in the European conflict dealt with the advance into Germany in 1944–1945. Churchill and Brooke backed General Bernard L.

"Monty" Montgomery in his desire to strike for Berlin in a single thrust by his XXI Army Group. Eisenhower, the supreme Allied theater commander-in-chief, had the support of FDR and the American chiefs in his insistence on a broad-front advance by all three of his Western Allied army groups and in his refusal to try to outrace the Soviet forces to Berlin. Many factors, particularly logistics and terrain, were involved in the final determination to let Eisenhower prevail on both issues.

British critics still cite these controversies as evidence of unimaginative, overcautious American operational thinking and nearsightedness at high levels, including naiveté toward impending postwar political crises. By the time the British succumbed on these matters, it was obvious they had lost their early favorable negotiating position. Their wisdom, based on nearly three years' experience fighting the Axis, and their superior military strength over the Americans for almost two years after Pearl Harbor, had earned the British the senior role during the formative years of the Anglo-American coalition. But in light of the overwhelming dominance of American manpower and firepower in the final operations of the war, Churchill and his chiefs were compelled to acknowledge America's superior voice in Anglo-American strategy.

The Soviet Union was a puzzling and ambivalent factor in the determination of Anglo-American strategy. In a positive sense, Stalin's forces were vital in tying down huge numbers of German ground and air units from the dark days of 1941–1942 on the Eastern Front to the overwhelming Soviet successes of 1944–1945. On the negative side, the Combined Chiefs of Staff were deeply concerned in the first year or so of the Soviet-German war that the Soviet military would be defeated. Until near the end of the European conflict in 1945, the Western Allies feared that Stalin might then negotiate a separate peace with Hitler, gaining territorial concessions in East Europe and elsewhere that the Anglo-American leaders would not have wished to grant.

Worse still, the Soviets might have been forced by continued military disasters to enter into an alliance with Germany.

Washington and London saw it as imperative that the Soviets be kept in the fight against the Germans and that Lend-Lease continue to flow in order to ensure operational successes on the Eastern Front. Stalin maintained an ongoing quarrel with Roosevelt and Churchill over promised aid that was late or sunk by U-boats as well as over the continuing postponement of the Second Front, which would bring genuine relief to his embattled forces by drawing enemy divisions westward. At Tehran in late 1943, Stalin was the prime instigator of the final agreement to the plan for the invasion of Normandy by stubbornly demanding to be informed of the assault date (and its commander). In spite of problems with the Big Three alliance, notably the lack of Soviet cooperation in strategic planning and in breaking its relations with Japan until the last week of the war, the destruction wrought by Soviet ground and air forces along their two-thousand-mile front made the Western Allied operations in the Mediterranean and Northwest Europe immeasurably more effective. This was especially true of the giant Soviet offensive timed to support the Normandy invasion.

On the other side of the world, meanwhile, compromise prevailed also in Allied strategy-making in the war with Japan. This version of give-and-take was not mainly between the Americans and their Allied partners in that conflict; it involved MacArthur and his American army-dominated headquarters and, on the other hand, Nimitz and his American navy-controlled headquarters. In March 1942, after MacArthur arrived in Australia from the Philippines, he publicly proclaimed that President Roosevelt had ordered him to go to Australia "for the purpose, as I understand it, of organizing the American offensive against Japan, a primary object of which is the relief of the Philippines. I came through and I shall return."

Actually, neither FDR nor the Joint Chiefs envisioned at

that moment a MacArthur-led advance from Australia to Tokyo. American war planners had long predicted that an armed clash between America and Japan would be primarily a naval war. In part because of the disappointingly slow and costly American reconquest of Papua in New Guinea and Guadalcanal in the Solomon Islands, the Joint Chiefs decided at the Quebec Conference in August 1943 to authorize Nimitz to launch a second axis of advance, spearheaded by his navy and marine forces in the Central Pacific. MacArthur protested in vain, and, beginning with Nimitz's invasion of the Gilbert Islands in November 1943, the Joint Chiefs gave priority to the Central Pacific in the war with Japan.

An interesting compromise that pitted the two Pacific theater commanders against the Joint Chiefs involved their respective plans to assault the two principal Japanese strongholds that lay in their paths—Rabaul on New Britain, targeted early by MacArthur, and Truk in the Caroline Islands, eyed by Nimitz. The Joint Chiefs eventually decided that both Rabaul and Truk could be bypassed, but in turn they agreed to provide additional forces to envelop and isolate those two most powerful Japanese bases in the West Pacific. The decision was undoubtedly a wise one, though MacArthur strongly opposed it for a while.

Another compromise in the Pacific war related to the principle of unity of command. Soon after the Joint Chiefs established MacArthur's and Nimitz's theaters, the outspoken Southwest Pacific commander began a gradually accelerating campaign to change the JCS decision. His criticism mounted especially after the great naval battle for Leyte Gulf in November 1944. The American Third and Seventh fleets eventually won at Leyte, but their poor coordination almost led to disaster. MacArthur attributed these mistakes to miscommunications because the Third Fleet reported to Nimitz at Pearl Harbor while the Seventh Fleet was under the Southwest Pacific general, who was on Leyte in the Philippines. After the war MacArthur declared:

"Of all the faulty decisions of the war, perhaps the most inexplicable one was the failure to unify the command in the Pacific.... It resulted in divided effort, the waste of diffusion and duplication of force, [and] undue extension of the war with added casualties and cost."

MacArthur does not add, however, that he would have tolerated a unified command only if *he* had been the officer selected. He presented a command dilemma for the JCS since he had been the army chief of staff in 1930–1935 when Marshall and Arnold were quite inferior in rank; and throughout the Pacific conflict MacArthur was the senior Allied officer. King, Nimitz, and virtually all the navy's senior admirals adamantly opposed the placement of the Pacific Fleet entirely under MacArthur's command or, in fact, under any American army or Allied officer.

The weakness of Japan's war machine in comparison with Germany's, and the far greater expanse of the Japanese empire to be defended, made it possible for American strategists to compromise on the principle of unity of command in that conflict. As it was, MacArthur's and Nimitz's offensives were effective one-two punches that kept the Japanese off balance. The JCS thus allowed the issue of unified command in the Pacific to drift unsettled until hostilities ended.

If one word could be chosen to describe the most significant factor in Allied operational successes, it would be "logistics." Problems of supply, maintenance, and distribution, along with the priority and allocation of units and war materiel, consumed countless hours in the work of theater commanders and their military superiors. From the early months of the war to the final days, they were plagued by recurring shortages in certain logistical areas, notably shipping, landing craft, and service troops. In a global war involving unprecedented distances between bases of operations and combat zones, there were also continual problems of securing lines of supply and communication. The Battle of the Atlantic, for example, became a desperate struggle affecting logistical lifelines not only to Britain and the Soviet Union but also to China and Australia. Especially before American production of war materiel became abundant, the huge losses of weapons and supplies aboard Allied ships torpedoed in the Atlantic meant that future monthly quotas of such items for lower-priority theaters had to be scaled down, often drastically, to make up for needs on the Soviet front and other higher-priority combat zones. As the war wore on and the campaigns grew larger, the demand for support and service units competed with the need for more combat personnel. After the Second World War, all the war colleges of the major powers made certain that future military leaders were educated in logistics as a cardinal factor in war.

In earlier conflicts, intelligence about the enemy had been gathered in the field, and usually its uses had been determined by senior field commanders. Such was the case with reconnaissance, spies, and resistance groups in occupied countries. By the time of World War II, communications (radio) intelligence had become quite advanced, and military experts in codes and ciphers were achieving far-reaching successes, particularly in America and Britain. With the formation of the Combined Chiefs of Staff and its Combined Intelligence Committee, the two nations began an unprecedented sharing of secrets. The American army's Signal Intelligence Service, for instance, shared with their British counterparts the Magic process of breaking Purple, the complicated Japanese cipher for high-level diplomatic radio traffic. The British, on the other hand, made available their Ultra device which had penetrated the radio signals of the Germans' Enigma machine.

In 1942 American cryptographers made important breakthroughs on Japanese navy codes and ciphers, while the next year the Americans solved the Japanese army's main communication signals. Although of little value in averting the Japanese attack on Hawaii that brought the United States into war in December 1941, both Magic and Ultra-J (the designation for American intercepts of Japanese military and naval radio traffic) were immensely helpful later. In the Pacific, American communications intelligence was indispensable to the naval victory at Midway in June 1942, the ambush of Admiral Isoru Yamamoto in a plane over Bougainville in March 1943, the conquest of Northeast New Guinea in 1944, and the devastating American submarine operations in 1943–1945. Cooperation with the British regarding Ultra in the war against Germany (often called Ultra-G by Americans) brought outstanding results in winning the Battle of the Atlantic by the autumn of 1943 and in successes in ground campaigns like the Allied invasion of South France in August 1944.

Communications intelligence, however, had its limitations. The Germans and Japanese never learned during the war about Allied breakthroughs on Purple and Enigma messages, mainly because of extreme Anglo-American security. This meant that sometimes Ultra knowledge could not be conveyed to forces in harm's way for fear of risking Ultra's disclosure. Limits were also imposed by the small number of persons on the distribution list of Ultra revelations. Certain senior commanders who had Ultra clearance, including MacArthur, Patton, and General Mark W. Clark of the U.S. Fifth Army in Italy, sometimes were inclined to disdain its reports in favor of the findings of their own intelligence chiefs. Magic, Ultra-J, and Ultra-G rarely provided more than a third of a particular enemy message in time to analyze it and make decisions that could affect operations.

Besides cryptographers and cryptanalysts in communications intelligence, the other principal American conveyors of intelligence data in World War II were aircraft, submarines, resistance fighters, and a unique organization in sabotage, espionage, and intelligence—the Office of Strategic Services, headed by Brigadier General William J. Donovan. OSS researchers, spies, and other field agents established a brilliant record. Their work marks another phase of Anglo-American cooperation, for the OSS and the British Special

Operations Executive generally worked well together and in coordination with underground movements, especially in the Low Countries, France, and Italy.

The American alliance with Britain was not without administrative and ethnocentric flaws, but it outshone the three Axis powers in achieving coordination at top staff levels, global planning, sharing of resources, and cooperation on both conventional and communications intelligence. If Germany, Japan, and Italy had realized such successful teamwork in these areas, the outcome of the Second World War might have been far different.

PART TWO

The War Against Germany and Italy

4

At Sea and in the Skies

NAVAL ACTIONS IN the Atlantic and air operations over Europe began with the German ground offensive in Poland in September 1939. By the time America entered World War II, the Atlantic engagements and the European air war were both mounting in intensity. Although the United States had wavered between neutrality and co-belligerency (short of large-scale commitment of combat personnel) during the twenty-seven months before December 1941, it had assisted in the naval and air defenses of beleaguered Britain in significant ways.

In September 1940 President Roosevelt signed an executive agreement with Churchill called the Destroyers-Bases Deal. To help the Royal Navy in its desperate fight against German U-boats to secure Atlantic sea lanes, fifty American destroyers of World War I vintage were given to the British in exchange for leases on naval and air bases and sites located in eight British possessions in the Western Hemisphere, stretching from Newfoundland to British Guiana in South America. The Lend-Lease Act in March 1941 permitted the shipment of war materiel and relief supplies from America to the United Kingdom and other nations designated by FDR, the grand total eventually exceeding $50 billion. The president signed agreements with the Danish government-in-exile for American forces to establish naval and air bases on Greenland the next month and on Iceland in July 1941.

Meanwhile, Roosevelt had authorized the strengthening of American naval forces in the Atlantic and their upgrading from squadron to fleet size, with aggressive Admiral Ernest King as commander of the new Atlantic Fleet. That April FDR approved King's use of his ships to escort Britain-bound convoys as far east as the twenty-sixth longitude, about midway across the Atlantic. King's fleet also began tracking and reporting German U-boats to the Royal Navy and Royal Air Force, the British usually responding quickly with strikes.

Many American media pundits suggested by late summer 1941 that the United States was on a collision course with Germany in the accelerating war in the Atlantic. Events in September were surely fraught with the danger of a full-scale conflict between the two countries. The USS Greer, a destroyer patrolling and tracking German submarines south of Iceland, was damaged by a U-boat it was following. Roosevelt reacted dramatically with a "shoot-on-sight" order to the Atlantic Fleet and warned German and Italian ships to stay out of American defensive waters, which he soon extended farther eastward to permit convoy duty by the American navy as far as Iceland.

In October tensions continued to rise as Roosevelt asked Congress to amend the Neutrality Act of 1939 to allow American merchant vessels to be armed and to sail through combat zones. Later that month two American destroyers were engaged by German submarines off Iceland: the Kearney was heavily damaged, and eleven American sailors were killed; two weeks later the Reuben James lost a hundred crewmen when it was sunk by a torpedo. FDR proclaimed with some hyperbole: "The shooting war has started" in the Atlantic. Congress responded in mid-November by approving the arming of American merchantmen and their passage through combat zones and to belligerent ports.

Following the Pearl Harbor attack in December, King was sent to Washington as commander of the United States Fleet; the next March he succeeded Admiral Harold Stark as chief of naval operations while continuing as overall head of the entire fleet and keeping a sharp interest in Atlantic operations. Admiral Royal E. Ingersoll became the new commander of the Atlantic Fleet, inheriting an antisubmarine situation that soon became nightmarish.

While American ship production was now growing fast, so were the sinkings of American and Allied ships. Most embarrassing for King and Ingersoll, many of the vessels were being torpedoed not far from the American coast— near New York City and Long Island, the Outer Banks of North Carolina, and southern Florida. U-boats, which were operating increasingly in organized groups, or "wolf packs," hovered off the resort cities of Florida, which rarely observed blackouts. Cargo ships often sailed past these resorts at night, but they were silhouetted by the bright city lights and became easy pickings. So many good targets were available that one submarine group commander ordered his captains to skip the vessels that seemed to be "riding high" as being empty or lightly loaded.

Rear Admiral Samuel E. Morison wrote: "The U-boat blitz gave the Gulf Sea Frontier the melancholy distinction of having the most sinkings in May 1942 (41 ships; 219,867 gross tons) of any one area in any month during the war." Oil refineries and other facilities along the shoreline of the Gulf of Mexico from Texas to Florida were shelled boldly by surfaced submarines, and several U-boats ventured up the mouth of the Mississippi River, though not to New Orleans. Not until 1943 was the Intercoastal Canal system fully operational. This was a route from Texas to the Northeast running along the coast and protected to seaward largely by offshore islands and reefs. The new system reduced the losses to submarines suffered by coastal shipping.

These audacious German submarine attacks, especially in the Gulf and East Coast regions, would seemingly have provoked serious criticism of King as the powerful and often arrogant naval chief, and of Ingersoll as the head of Atlantic operations. Somehow they both managed to retain their posts until the tide turned in the U-boat war and, indeed, until the end of the Second World War. Part of the reason for their survival lay in the confused situation of limited liability that prevailed because the American navy and army air forces did not early achieve unity of command in antisubmarine warfare. Another factor may have been the Pentagon's effectiveness in hiding from the public the success of the German submarines.

Disputes occurred between the admirals and air generals regarding patrol jurisdiction over different regions of the Gulf of Mexico and the West Atlantic. King, Arnold, and their staffs frequently clashed during the early months when sinkings of cargo ships in those areas occurred faster than new vessels could be built. The confused, stressful conditions were precipitated by differences over command organizations, tactics, and patrol and detection techniques, as well as jealous squabbles over which service would gain logistical priority to wage the antisubmarine war.

On an international level, naval and air authorities of the United States, Great Britain, and Canada, all of which had ships and aircraft involved in the Atlantic struggle, confronted each other with similar jurisdictional disputes. Some of their problems were solved or eased by allocating national responsibilities by geographic zones, though national disputes continued. When Admiral Dudley Pound, head of the Royal Navy, ordered Convoy PQ-17, en route to Russia in July 1942, to scatter under heavy attack, King severely criticized this abandonment of merchant ships by combat vessels, which cost sixteen of the twenty-two merchantmen. For a while King refused to cooperate further in combined convoys; ultimately he relented when the British agreed to maintain convoy security even under extreme stress.

In early 1943 King and Arnold finally reached a modus vivendi of sorts, with King obtaining principal authority over antisubmarine operations in the American zones. He then established the Tenth Fleet as his principal command to deal with the German submarine menace. Although King designated himself as the new fleet's commander, he delegated operational control to Rear Admiral Francis S. Low, chief of staff of the Tenth Fleet and a skilled submariner who, according to a fellow officer, "knew as much about King's way of thinking as anyone."

A decisive shift in favor of the Allies was not easily achieved. If May 1942 had been the worst month for Allied sinkings in the Gulf of Mexico, the first three weeks of March 1943 were the low point in the Atlantic and on the Arctic route around Scandinavia to the Soviet ports of Murmansk and Archangel. German planes, submarines, and even some surface ships swarmed out of the northern coastal regions of Norway to attack convoys with terrible tolls, sometimes sinking 70 percent or more of a convoy and putting sailors in frigid waters that made life brief unless rescue came quickly. Toward the end of March, however, according to British Brigadier Peter Young, "suddenly the escorts and ASW forces gained the upper hand. The factors were complex: the superior Anglo-American arrangements for the cooperation between scientists and the armed forces; the return of all the escorts and escort carriers diverted to Torch [the invasion of Northwest Africa, beginning in November 1942] and a change in the convoy cipher all played a part in preventing the U-boats from destroying the convoy system."

The change in fortunes was clearly evident when all the German submarines at sea were recalled for equipping with new devices, notably the *schnorchel*, an air mast which enabled submerged subs to recharge batteries. That summer, when most of the U-boats remained in or near their bases, Anglo-American air forces stationed in England launched an intensive campaign against U-boats in the Bay of Biscay and the U-boat pens along that southwestern coast of France. The now-weakened German air force, the Luftwaffe, sent fighters to confront the Allied planes, but they were too few to thwart attacks on the U-boats, whose destruction increased sharply by late summer.

The submarines were more menacing with their new

equipment when they returned in the latter part of 1943 to attacking convoys on the routes to Britain and Russia. But their new assets were more than offset by the greatly increased effectiveness of Anglo-American covering forces for the convoys. In addition, that autumn marked the virtual termination of German surface raiders as serious threats to Allied shipping; the last German heavy ship involved in the raiding, a battle cruiser, was destroyed that December. Later that year, Admiral King announced the turning point in the war in the Atlantic with the cautious assessment that German U-boats "have not been driven from the seas, but they have changed status from menace to problem."

The decline of the German navy was obvious in its virtual inability to interfere with the shipping required for the vast buildup for Operation Overlord, the Normandy assault, during the six months or so preceding the invasion in early June 1944. The change was even more evident in the inconsequential attempts by enemy aircraft and subs to thwart the cross-channel movement of Overlord men and materiel not only on D-day, June 6, but throughout the Normandy campaign the next two months.

Allied intelligence indicated that the Germans were working on several new types of submarines, some turbine-powered, that could wreak havoc anew on Allied shipping if unleashed. But from the fall of 1944 to the spring of 1945, Anglo-American ground forces overran German U-boat bases along the coasts of the Bay of Biscay in France and of the North Sea in the Low Countries and northwestern Germany, together with the principal German shipyards. And strategic bombing, if not as destructive as the Allies expected against the submarine pens and U-boat construction, had indirectly helped the antisubmarine war by damaging factories that produced key U-boat parts and weapons, including torpedoes. Also, by concentrating on Luftwaffe aircraft production, Allied long-range bombers had forced shifts in priorities from submarine to aircraft work that contributed to the problems of keeping U-boat construction under way, much less converting to the new turbine submarines.

The costs of the war in the Atlantic were staggering. Of more than 1,100 submarines employed by the German navy during the conflict, 781 were sunk. The Italian navy lost 21 submarines in the Atlantic and 64 elsewhere. Axis submarines, surface raiders, and aircraft, mostly German, used against Atlantic and Arctic shipping, destroyed more than 2,770 Allied ships, mostly Anglo-American merchantmen, totaling about 23 million tons. About 15,000 Americans were killed in the Atlantic conflict; British losses were 60,000, and the Germans lost 28,000 submariners alone and an unknown number of other personnel.

Admiral Morison called the German submarine operations "the greatest threat to Allied victory over the Axis." The Atlantic may have been the most significant theater logistically because the precious cargoes sunk there meant less American assistance not only for the chief beneficiaries of the Atlantic convoys, Britain and the Soviet Union, but also for all the rest of the Allies. Allocations of Lend-Lease materials, whether flour or machine guns, had to be scaled back temporarily despite impressive American agricultural and industrial outputs, so serious were the losses during the darkest phases of the Atlantic conflict. The failure of Roosevelt and Churchill to fulfill their pledges of aid to Stalin, which had to be routed mainly by sea and fell behind almost monthly for long periods, contributed strongly to Soviet distrust and to the wartime origins of the later East-West confrontation called the cold war.

Besides American naval assistance to Britain before December 1941, the United States also provided aircraft and ordnance. In his annual budget message to Congress in early January 1940, Roosevelt called for funds to build fifty thousand warplanes a year. General Arnold, head of the American army's air arm, was encouraged at first by the president's words, for he had been aggressively trying to build his forces. The sometimes impetuous Arnold was furious, however, when he learned that Roosevelt had worked out surreptitious agreements with the British and French governments for the purchase of new aircraft from manufacturers in the United States. These orders were to be given priority over deliveries to the American air corps, which was far short of combat planes. Arnold protested the secret deals in closed-door testimony before the House Military Affairs Committee in March 1940. An angry president summoned Arnold to the White House and told him that he was to cooperate or face a transfer to Guam.

In June 1940, $43 million in ground and air equipment from War Department stocks was sent to the United Kingdom. FDR increased such aid after the fall of France that month and through the ensuing aerial Battle of Britain. The inauguration of Lend-Lease the following spring brought a vast expansion of aid to Britain. The German invasion of the USSR in June 1941 soon meant large Lend-Lease deals with Stalin as well.

The secret Anglo-American military meetings in early 1941, which led to the ABC-1 report, also produced an understanding that large-scale strategic bombing would be an essential part of the Western Allies' future strategy against Germany. Many high-ranking British and American air leaders were convinced that such a campaign could make massive ground operations on the European continent unnecessary. Through 1941, however, the Royal Air Force Bomber Command had generally demonstrated that, even with impending American support, strategic bombing would probably produce prohibitive losses for the attackers, minor or no damage to factories, submarine pens, and other key "hardened" targets, and disappointingly little demoralization of the Germans' spirit.

In the spring of 1942 the U.S. Eighth Air Force began gradually moving to England. It was headed by Arnold's longtime comrades, Major General Carl A. "Tooey" Spaatz as commander and Brigadier General Ira C. Eaker as deputy. They arrived with only a small advance contingent of aircraft, including some B-17 heavy bombers. By then the RAF had shifted to less costly night operations, and the British found Spaatz and Eaker agreeable to committing their bombers to precision daylight raids. The early missions by the Eighth Air Force were small, with heavier losses in planes and crews than the Americans had anticipated. It was soon obvious that the Eighth would have to be considerably strengthened to be of much help to Air Marshal Arthur T. Harris's RAF Bomber Command. The Luftwaffe and the German antiaircraft system proved as formidable to the American newcomers as they had to the RAF since 1939.

Neither the American nor British air leaders were deterred in their convictions that a more massive and better-protected strategic bombing program could force Germany's capitulation. Roosevelt and Churchill were not as enthusiastic, but at the Casablanca Conference in January 1943 they and the Combined Chiefs of Staff were persuaded by the American and British "bomber barons" to establish Operation Pointblank, or the Combined Bomber Offensive, as a high priority in the war against Germany. According to the Combined Chiefs, its purpose was "the progressive destruction and dislocation of the enemy's war industrial and economic system and the undermining of his morale to the point where his capacity for armed resistance is fatally weakened." They did not see strategic air power as a war-winning weapon but predicted cautiously that Pointblank "will have an increasing effect on the enemy's distributive system and industrial potential." Evidencing more confidence in it than either man really felt, Roosevelt and Churchill claimed in a message to Stalin that Pointblank would be a "second front in the air." The Soviet leader expressed no more pleasure than he had the previous November when the Allies had tried to pass off the invasion of Northwest Africa as a second front that would help Soviet forces.

The launching of Pointblank had to be delayed because most of the American air strength in the British Isles had

been shifted to Northwest Africa to support Operation
Torch. In fact, Eaker, who now commanded the Eighth Air
Force, had barely enough planes—primarily medium bombers and fighters—to carry out small missions against limited
targets near the coast of Northwest Europe. They initially
concentrated on railyards, air and naval bases, and U-boat
bases.

Beginning in mid-August 1943 Eaker changed his priority
to the enemy aircraft industry far deeper inland, for he had
recently obtained additional groups of heavy bombers. The
first long-distance raids into Germany were against aircraft and ball-bearing manufacturers in Regensburg and
Schweinfurt. On those two missions the Luftwaffe and
antiaircraft guns destroyed 60 of the 315 B-17s. Against
Stuttgart the following month the Eighth Bomber Command lost 45 of 262 B-17s. These and further deep raids
were conducted without fighter escorts because no fighters
then available had the necessary range. Crews and planes
were being destroyed at such an appalling rate that morale
in the Eighth Air Force began to drop sharply, and Arnold
developed doubts about Eaker's leadership. In October,
Eaker sent his heavy-bomber groups, now reinforced with
planes from Northwest Africa, to hit important targets deep
in Germany again. The low point came in mid-October
when 60 of 230 B-17s were lost on another attack on
Schweinfurt, and 138 of the remaining 170 bombers suffered
casualties and damage. Eaker was forced to call off further
long-distance missions. In December he was replaced by
Major General James H. Doolittle and was sent to head
Mediterranean Allied Air Forces—a much less significant
command in his and most airmen's eyes.

As Eaker departed from England, however, the tide was
about to turn. Aircraft production in the United States
was nearing its peak, and the Eighth Air Force was
finally receiving not only the quantity of heavy bombers it
needed but also large numbers of an excellent new long-
range fighter, the North American P-51. The Eighth soon

mounted its first six-hundred-plane mission and, with P-51s as escorts, suffered relatively minor losses. Meanwhile, in Italy, the U.S. Fifteenth Air Force, led by Major General Nathan F. Twining, was striking targets far into Germany and East Europe. Back in England, Spaatz became the head of United States Strategic Air Forces, Europe, with control over all American strategic air missions in the war against Germany.

In February 1944 the Eighth Air Force attacked Schweinfurt for the third time and lost just 11 of 231 bombers. During the final week of that month, six large American bombing missions were sent deep into Germany. Their bombing results were better, their losses negligible, and their fighter escorts deadly against Luftwaffe interceptors. Soon Germany began to experience a critical shortage of skilled pilots. The Germans were still capable of fierce air and ground resistance against bombing missions, but, as one authority observes, "the Americans could now make the losses good in planes and crews, and the Germans could not."

During the five months preceding the Normandy invasion of June 1944, General Eisenhower won a difficult battle against the Anglo-American bomber barons. Grudgingly they yielded to his plan to shift their heavy bombers from raids against distant vital centers in Germany to missions against closer transportation and tactical targets that would isolate the Normandy region and hinder German reinforcements when the Overlord invaders landed.

Once Normandy was secured later that summer, the Eighth and Fifteenth air forces returned to their strategic pounding of the German homeland. By December 1944 their raids often numbered two thousand aircraft. By then the cumulative impact of Pointblank was being felt by the German economy. The intensification was especially destructive during the final ten months of the war in Europe when 72 percent of the 2.7 million tons of bombs dropped on Germany during the war fell on that devastated nation. The worst impact was on large cities, not necessarily because of their concentration of military targets.

The two largest bombing efforts of the war were combined Anglo-American missions covering several days each against Hamburg and Dresden, Germany. The first was left in ruins after two days and two nights of continuous bombing by thousands of American and British heavies. A fire storm, moving faster than residents could flee, swept across more than half the city, wiping out 300,000 structures and killing between 60,000 and 100,000 people. By early 1945 Spaatz and Eaker found few worthy targets left for their big bombers. Harris proposed and Spaatz agreed to one last "big raid," this finale to be delivered against Dresden, one of Europe's most beautiful, historic, and least militarily significant cities. In mid-February British and American bombers attacked in force, alternating with night and day missions until the horrible fire storms erupted as at Hamburg. The city was all but wiped out, and more than 60,000 people died.

Operation Pointblank cost the American Eighth and Fifteenth air forces almost 5,000 heavy bombers and more than 40,000 crew members. The RAF Bomber Command paid even higher prices: 10,000 heavy bombers and 47,000 personnel. German civilian and military deaths from the bombing missions were enormous: at least 300,000 civilians died; military losses also were staggering in ground and air personnel.

Although the Soviet air force was deadly in tactical, or air-ground, support, its strategic bombers did not attempt a deep-ranging campaign against Central European targets similar to Pointblank. Under the leadership of Major General John R. Deane, head of the American Military Mission in Moscow, repeated attempts were made to negotiate a "shuttle-bombing" program whereby American long-range bombers could greatly expand their bomb loads and range by using Soviet bases in Eastern Europe. This would allow American (and possibly British) heavy bombers to stage from their bases in the United Kingdom and Italy, attack targets deep in Central or Eastern Europe, and continue on to advance Soviet bases for refueling and rearming. They could then make additional bomb runs on their way back to their bases in Britain and Italy. Finally the Soviets, ever secretive about Westerners entering their military installations, agreed to a very limited shuttle-bombing program that lasted from June to September 1944. The Western Allied air crews that landed at Soviet airfields were regarded suspiciously and their movements were carefully restricted. The project was terminated in September with mutual recriminations about who was to blame for its stoppage.

From the Western perspective it was obvious that the Soviets were intensely distrustful, and some historians later date the origins of the cold war from this and other breakdowns in communication and cooperation in 1944. Were it not for these mutual suspicions, the shuttle-bombing experiment might have greatly augmented the aims of Pointblank and pointed the way to other potentially fruitful coordination in air and ground operations. Stalin and his chiefs failed to appreciate the mutual advantages, while East-West tensions on other matters worsened for want of compromise and mutual trust.

In contrast to the war in the Atlantic, where Allied casualties were borne as the horrendous cost of securing lines of communication and did not precipitate much subsequent criticism of their necessity, Operation Pointblank has been debated heatedly ever since the war. Its limited effectiveness against Germany's economy, military establishment, and morale has been weighed often and found wanting by many critics, some of whom also point out ethical questions raised by such deliberate destruction of civilians and nonmilitary targets. Whatever the liabilities of Pointblank, and they are many, the Allied strategic bombing program had a powerful, if not decisive, influence on Germany's capitulation.

5

Learning from Torch and Husky

AMERICA'S FIRST GROUND campaigns against the Axis were led by two future five-star generals, Douglas Mac-Arthur in the Pacific and Dwight Eisenhower in the Mediterranean. After MacArthur moved to Australia in March 1942 to organize a new Allied theater command, his successor in the defense of the Philippines, Major General Jonathan M. Wainwright, was soon compelled to surrender the American-Filipino army. It was beaten by a Japanese force half its size. American soldiers' baptism of fire against the European Axis came later that year. Eisenhower did not lose an army in Northwest Africa, but his and his troops' achievements were disappointing. In Tunisia an American corps was badly defeated at Kasserine Pass in its first encounter with German soldiers. In the ensuing campaign in Sicily, Eisenhower's longtime buddy George Patton was allowed to forsake the pre-assault plan and instead won personal glory and lots of headlines by dashing to Palermo in Northwest Sicily and then to Messina on the northeast coast. Meanwhile, the bulk of the German troops defending Sicily were permitted to avoid entrapment and to escape to South Italy to engage the Western Allies soon again. Looking at the records of MacArthur and Eisenhower in their first campaigns, no one could have predicted their enormous successes later in the war. To the contrary, initial American ground operations in the Pacific and the Mediterranean portended a long, long war.

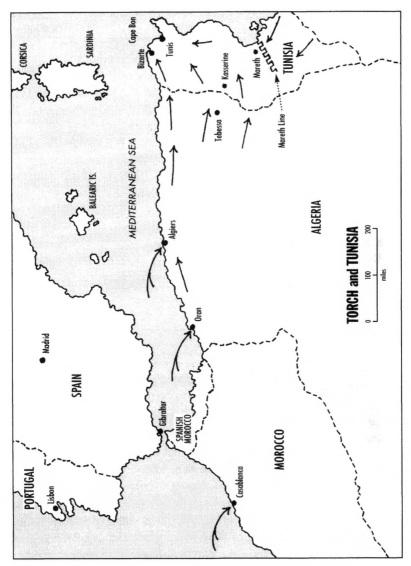

TORCH and TUNISIA

CORSICA

SARDINIA

Cape Bon

Bizerte

Tunis

Kasserine

Mareth

TUNISIA

Tebessa

Mareth Line

MEDITERRANEAN SEA

BALEARIC IS.

Algiers

ALGERIA

Oran

Madrid

SPAIN

Gibraltar

SPANISH MOROCCO

MOROCCO

Casablanca

PORTUGAL

Lisbon

0   100   200

miles

Churchill and his military chiefs had promoted Gymnast, a plan for an invasion of Algeria, ever since the British had rushed to Washington for the first Anglo-American summit shortly after Pearl Harbor. By mid-summer 1942 Churchill had won over FDR on Gymnast despite strong opposition from the American Joint Chiefs, particularly Marshall. It will be recalled that the JCS favored a cross-channel invasion of France as soon as feasible. According to the Joint Chiefs, Gymnast, or Torch, as the operation was renamed in the summer of 1942, would be tangential to the primary aim of a climactic, decisive collision with the Germans. Besides, it would not satisfy Stalin's call for a second front to draw German divisions away from the Eastern Front. The JCS was correct on both counts, but the British still retained the upper hand in the higher direction of the Western Allies' strategy. They were generous in giving Eisenhower the supreme Allied command of Torch, but British officers would be the senior commanders of all the major forces. In the plan that eventually evolved as Operation Torch, the British agreed to add an American-favored assault on French Morocco.

The outstanding good fortune of the Torch forces was the passage of the Western Task Force, which transported a corps headed by Major General George Patton, from the United States to French Morocco without losing any ships in the U-boat-infested waters of the North Atlantic. On November 8, 1942, the Torch invasion began with at least eight separate landings: three by Patton's troops, the largest aimed at Casablanca; three by the Central Task Force in the vicinity of Oran, Algeria, spearheaded by American troops under Major General Lloyd R. Fredendall; and the Eastern Task Force's two landings on each side of Algiers by British and American troops under U.S. Major General Charles W. Ryder. The Central and Eastern Forces had come from England. The planners had long believed that letting the Americans predominate in the initial assaults would make French resistance more brief-lived, given the strain in Anglo-French relations after the German-dominated puppet regime had been established at Vichy.

Three days after the assault landings, French defenses crumbled at Casablanca, Oran, and Algiers, along with lesser French strongholds. The Vichy government severed diplomatic relations with the United States the day after Torch began, and German forces took control of "unoccupied" Vichy France while German reinforcements were quickly sent to Tunisia. Meanwhile, in Algiers, French Admiral Jean Darlan turned against Hitler and Vichy. Thanks to diplomatic efforts by Eisenhower, his Torch deputy Major General Mark W. Clark, and Robert D. Murphy of the State Department, French leaders in Algeria and Morocco began to cooperate politically and militarily in maintaining order and providing troops for the forthcoming showdown with the Axis in Tunisia. Some American and British media criticized Eisenhower for negotiating with Vichy collaborators, but the arrangement undoubtedly saved many American lives. Admiral Darlan, widely viewed by the Western press as the most infamous of the deal-makers, was mysteriously assassinated that Christmas Eve.

The Torch planners had hoped Eisenhower's troops could seize Tunisia before the Germans could move large forces and defensive works there. Unfortunately, Eisenhower held back considerable strength along the border of Algeria and Spanish Morocco in order to protect his rear if the Germans made a sudden advance through Spain. In addition, Lieutenant General Kenneth A. N. Anderson, head of the British First Army, which was the principal Torch unit, was slowed by heavy rains, strong German air attacks, and ferocious resistance by the advance elements of the Fifth Panzer Army of General Jürgen von Arnim. By the beginning of 1943 von Arnim's army was at full strength and holding its own against the British First Army in northern and central Tunisia. Besides his largely British troops, Anderson also commanded two units attached to his First Army: a French corps and Fredendall's II Corps, the latter being the largest American ground unit in Torch.

Meanwhile, the contenders in the old desert war in Egypt and Libya had arrived at the southern border of Tunisia, where the German-Italian forces had taken positions along the well-fortified Mareth Line. Field Marshal Erwin Rommel's Afrika Korps, together with attached Italian units, had made the long retreat after its defeat at El Alamein, Egypt, the previous November. Pursuing Rommel in an inexplicably plodding manner was General Bernard Montgomery's British Eighth Army. Until late February, von Arnim and Rommel, with strong Luftwaffe support, were able to keep Anderson and Montgomery from linking up in the heart of Tunisia.

On February 14 the battle of Kasserine Pass began between Rommel's Afrika Korps and Fredendall's II Corps. Rommel launched a surprise assault against the green Americans, apparently intending to capture the big Allied supply depot nearby at Tebessa. The German troops had excellent air support and overwhelming armor. Fredendall was unaggressive and only slowly comprehended the situation. Luckily for him and his men, von Arnim did not launch a supporting attack to the north as Rommel had expected. On the other hand, Anderson was tardy in realizing the breakthrough Rommel had achieved and failed to dispatch reinforcements to the Americans. On February 22 Rommel, encountering stronger resistance to the west and realizing von Arnim was not coming to his support, skillfully withdrew his panzers all the way back to the Mareth Line. The next day he received word from Hitler that he would be the overall commander in Tunisia. The badly mangled II Corps was fortunate that Rommel had not held such authority earlier.

The American setback at Kasserine Pass prompted a much needed reorganization of Allied forces. British General Harold L. Alexander was placed in command of the newly formed XVIII Army Group, which included the two British armies and the attached French and American units. Patton was given command of the demoralized II Corps, which he rapidly reenergized and moved to the counterattack. About the same time in early March that Patton began his aggressive actions, Rommel, who was ill, was pulled out of Tunisia, and von Arnim succeeded to overall command. General Gustav von Vaerst took charge of the Fifth Panzer Army in the north, while on the Mareth Line, Italian General Giovanni

Messe of the Italian First Army assumed command of a mixed Italian-German force.

In late March the initiative passed to the Allies. The British Eighth Army broke through the Mareth Line, the American II Corps linked up with Montgomery's northward advancing troops in early April, and the German Fifth Panzer Army slowly withdrew toward the main ports of Bizerte and Tunis. The final Allied offensive took place from April 22 to May 11. After about a month with the reinvigorated II Corps, Patton had returned to French Morocco to organize the U.S. Seventh Army for the July invasion of Sicily. His successor over the II Corps was Major General Omar N. Bradley, an old friend of both Patton and Eisenhower. During the final push in Tunisia the II Corps was outstanding, and Bradley demonstrated high-command potential. On May 7 the Americans captured Bizerte, while on the same day the British took Tunis. Cape Bon Peninsula was the last defensive position of the German and Italian forces. The bag of Axis prisoners was enormous: 275,000 German and Italian troops. American casualties from the Torch landings through Tunisia numbered 18,500.*

The Northwest Africa campaign had introduced Eisenhower, his American subordinates, and their troops to the vaunted German war machine. Its commanders were crafty and aggressive, its fighting men were rugged and full of spirit, and its weapons killed with awesome effectiveness. The campaign indicated that British caution in tackling powerful German forces was not unfounded.

In the drive from Casablanca to Bizerte, though it took a disappointing six months to complete, Eisenhower and his American superiors found that the stresses of war brought into sharp focus the commanders who would be needed for bigger battles. The action in Tunisia clearly showed that two

---

*Except when specific types of casualties are mentioned, hereafter the term "casualties" refers to military personnel killed, wounded, missing, and captured. Noncombatant military casualties, such as injured and sick, are identified separately.

American commanders would be counted upon heavily: Patton and Bradley.

While the Northwest African campaign was narrowing to a climactic fight for Tunisia, Anglo-American leaders met at the Casablanca Conference in January 1943. Roosevelt and the American Joint Chiefs could not match their British counterparts in amassing facts and arguments for their strategic views. The results were more compromises that seemed finally to be British negotiating triumphs. One of these Casablanca victories for the British was the decision to postpone a cross-channel invasion of France until 1944 and instead to assault Sicily (and, by implication, to consider Italy next). In return, the United States would be able to commit more of its forces against Japan, and, to Admiral King's delight, to launch a Central Pacific offensive that was expected to surpass MacArthur's Southwest Pacific drive in the dual advance toward Japan.

The command structure for Operation Husky, the Sicilian invasion, was a compromise by the Combined Chiefs of Staff, who named Eisenhower as the Allied supreme commander. As in Torch, British officers were chosen for the senior commands of Allied ground, sea, and air forces. Alexander would head the XV Army Group, which would consist of Montgomery's British Eighth Army spearheading the thrust northward along the east coast of Sicily and Patton's U.S. Seventh Army advancing parallel to the west and providing flank protection for the principal push by the British.

In a gambit that had its Hollywood aspects, the Allies left a corpse on a Spanish beach with documents stating that the next major invasion would be Greece, with only a feint at Sicily. Hitler was duped and rushed reinforcements to Greece, but Field Marshal Albert Kesselring, who was in charge of German defenses in South Italy, felt otherwise and sent additional troops into Sicily, including the outstanding Hermann Goering Panzer Division. The Axis senior commander in Sicily when the Husky operation began in July was Italian General Alfredo Guzzoni, head of the Italian Sixth Army. He had about 350,000 Italian and German troops, but the only first-class fighting men were the 60,000 Germans, who were defending the eastern part of Sicily. After the Allied triumph in Tunisia, American and British bombers daily attacked enemy military targets, especially airfields, in Sicily, Sardinia, and South Italy, as well as several tiny islands on the prospective route of the Husky armada. Pantelleria, one of these small islands with a weak Italian garrison, actually surrendered before Allied ground troops assaulted it. Strategic air power enthusiasts like Arnold and Spaatz must have been delighted, but Pantelleria's capitulation due to bombing alone turned out to be a unique occurrence. By July 10, when the Husky forces invaded, virtually all Axis aircraft on Sicily had been destroyed or withdrawn. This proved misleading, however, because German aircraft from bases in Italy were surprisingly destructive during the Sicilian operations.

The Husky armada comprised the Western Task Force, which included Patton's Seventh Army, and the Eastern Task Force, which transported Montgomery's Eighth Army. Unlike the long, submarine-menaced routes that the Torch forces followed from America and Britain to Northwest Africa, the Husky task forces were mounted from Tunisia, only 150 miles south of Sicily. They did run into stormy seas, however, which threw many ships off course. The troops of the American Seventh Army were landed on the southern coast at and around the port of Gela, while the British went ashore at two locations below Syracuse on the southeast tip of the island. Initial resistance by the enemy was lighter than expected, possibly because an invasion was not anticipated in such inclement weather. If reports of early ground action were generally favorable, disquieting news came on the evening of July 11, when two large formations of transport planes flew from Tunisia to drop their loads of paratroopers behind the American and British beachheads. At each site, tragedies of friendly fire occurred. Near Gela in the American sector, 144 transports were shot at by the Seventh Army and the fleet; 23 of the planes were downed, many of the others suffered heavy damage, and American casualties exceeded 150.

Patton had reason to be nervous about his Gela foothold, because that area was defended by the two finest divisions that Kesselring had deployed to Sicily. The absence of expected Allied close air support and the Luftwaffe's persistent raiding delayed the Americans from striking boldly inland above Gela. Soon large numbers of German tanks entered the fray, and numerous German counterattacks were repulsed, but at high cost. On July 13 the Americans got some relief: unknown to them, Kesselring and Guzzoni had agreed to shift their main firepower to the British front, which now lay in a plain along the east coast. The dominant terrain feature, controlled by the Axis, was the 10,900-foot volcano Mount Etna with its surrounding rugged ground. The Axis now placed top priority on retaining the high ground west and north of the British and keeping the Eighth Army squeezed into the low country along the coast. The enemy was determined that Montgomery's advance to Messina on the northeast tip of the island would be slow and bloody.

Meanwhile, Patton had fast become restless with his British-ordained fate to protect Montgomery's flank. After several overtures to Alexander regarding what he could do if unleashed, Patton was authorized on July 17 to strike out for Palermo, a move that might take pressure off the beleaguered Eighth Army. If ever an army commander possessed the leaders capable of undertaking a lightning thrust across the island, Patton had them in his two corps commanders, Bradley and Major General Geoffrey Keyes, along with perhaps the American army's finest division commander, Major General Lucian K. Truscott. While Montgomery's troops were stopped by savage German resistance, particularly from the Goering Division, Patton's Seventh Army advanced to the northwest coast, covering about

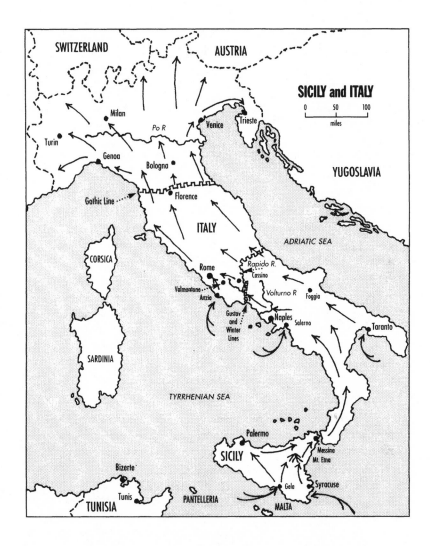

SICILY and ITALY

0   50   100
miles

twenty-five miles a day and seizing Palermo on July 22.
Truscott's crack Third Infantry Division had led the way.

Patton now received permission from Alexander to turn
eastward along the northern coast and drive to Messina,
which was still Montgomery's goal as well. Kesselring now
deployed several more German divisions to thwart the Americans' advance. Truscott's men continued to spearhead the
Seventh Army's offensive. As the augmented German de-

fenses slowed the Americans, Patton became somewhat over-eager to take Messina before the British; he launched several ill-conceived amphibious assaults along the northern coast. They were ineffective in accelerating the advance and indeed were risky ventures that more alert German coastal defenses could have turned into disasters.

During the latter part of July, along with the rein-forcements he had sent to Sicily, Kesselring had transferred there an unusually gifted officer, General Hans V. Hube, to head the XIV Panzer Corps. The new senior German leader in Sicily realized that the superior strength of the Allies made it impossible for him to defend Sicily successfully. Instead, Hube was bent on delaying the American and British armies as long as possible and on conducting an orderly evacuation of his forces from Sicily to Italy across the Strait of Messina, which ranged from two to ten miles in width. Hube distinguished himself as a master of withdrawal tactics: between August 3 and 17, 100,000 troops and 10,000 vehicles escaped across the Messina Strait.

On the 17th Sicily was declared secured after Patton's troops won the race to Messina, which brought the Seventh Army commander much publicity. But the campaign has left a number of troubling questions. Why was not the over-whelming naval and air strength of the Allies concentrated on the Strait of Messina during Hube's evacuation? If Patton had been compelled to adhere to the original plan and had provided strong flank support to Montgomery, might not the advance along the east coast to Messina have been swift enough to entrap the Axis forces on the island?

American casualties in the conquest of Sicily were 9,800. The Seventh Army had performed well, its troops demon-strating aggressiveness, tenacity, bravery, and fighting ability that gained the respect of the British and the enemy. On the other hand, General W. G. F. Jackson, a British authority on the campaign, observes that "the sterling qualities of the Germans in defense and withdrawal" were a forewarning that "the soft underbelly of Europe [Churchill's phrase] might turn into a crocodile's tail"—which was soon what happened in the Italian campaign. Hanson W. Baldwin, a respected American military analyst, was not as impressed by Patton's dash to Palermo and Messina as were many awed contemporary observers. Instead he found that the "sheer weight of men and metal overpowered the Germans in Sicily," and the German escape from the island "proved once again the strength of the German Army and its thorough training and high degree of professionalism."

For Patton, the Sicily campaign was a time of glory and sadness. Near the end of the fighting he inflicted a "crippling indignity" upon two wounded American soldiers and upon himself. He slapped them in separate incidents at military hospitals in Sicily. Both were hospitalized with combat fatigue (shock), but Patton misjudged and condemned them as cowards. Later he publicly apologized to them and to the Seventh Army. Eisenhower and Marshall left Patton on Sicily, in charge of a small garrison, while his colleagues moved up fast: General Clark was given the Fifth Army for the Italian campaign, General Bradley got the First Army and XII Army Group for the Normandy-to-Germany operations, and other friends received choice assignments. Finally, after leaving him in exile on Sicily for nearly five months, Eisenhower ordered Patton to England where he would ultimately head the Third Army in his greatest command performance. Bradley, Eisenhower, and Marshall all knew Patton well: they handled him exactly right to get the maximum out of this impetuous, aggressive fighter when it counted most.

Arguments persist over the conduct of Allied operations in Sicily, but, however flawed, they did win control of the island and contributed significantly to the downfall of the government that had taken Italy into the war on the Axis side. During the conquest of Sicily, Eisenhower and Clark had been engaged in secret negotiations with Italian leaders. In late July, Premier Benito Mussolini had been forced from power, but Marshal Pietro Badoglio, also a fascist but more moderate, succeeded him. Badoglio soon opened communications with the Allies for terms of surrender. Since the Anglo-Americans planned to launch amphibious landings along the western and southern coasts of South Italy in early September, it was imperative to try to keep Hitler from learning of the peace talks and from quickly sending large German forces into South Italy. On September 8 it was publicly proclaimed that Italy accepted the terms of unconditional surrender; Clark's Fifth Army began landing below Naples that same day. Unfortunately, Kesselring again had correctly anticipated the move, and the Allies found that Italian weapons and defenses had been quickly taken over by the far more dangerous Germans. All the lessons that the Allied participants in Torch and Husky had learned about war would be severely tested in the long and disappointing campaign for Italy they now faced.

6

The Hard Underbelly: Italy

WHEN THE DECISION was made at Casablanca in January 1943 to invade Sicily, a subsequent assault on Italy was implicit. Sicily was a province of Italy, and only the narrow Strait of Messina separated it from the Italian boot. At the Trident Conference in Washington, in May 1943, the British chiefs pushed for a plan for moving on to southern Italy after the conquest of Sicily. Agreement was not reached on an invasion of the Italian peninsula until July.

The American chiefs were not altogether pleased with this additional commitment in the Mediterranean, which they suspected was linked to Churchill's designs to further British imperialism and eventually send Anglo-American armies into the Danube and Balkan regions to thwart the Red Army's penetration into Central Europe. But the Americans went along with the involvement in Italy because they got something of a compromise at Trident: a British agreement at last on a firm date for the Normandy invasion, in May 1944, and an acceleration of American efforts in the war against Japan. Shortly after Trident adjourned, an Anglo-American planning staff was established in London for Operation Overlord, the future cross-channel invasion.

The command structure for operations in Italy followed the now familiar pattern: Eisenhower as supreme Allied commander, with the British as heads of the ground, sea, and air commands. Alexander continued as commander of the XV Army Group, which consisted of the American Fifth Army of General Mark Clark and the British Eighth Army of General Montgomery.

The Italian invasion began with Montgomery's forces crossing the Strait of Messina on September 3 and moving north against little resistance. Six days later a British amphibious assault captured Taranto, the main Italian naval base. From there elements of the Eighth Army advanced northward along the Adriatic side of the peninsula; on September 27 they seized Foggia and its large complex of air bases, which were soon expanded and heavily used by British and American aircraft. The two-pronged offensive by Montgomery had begun auspiciously, partly because of weak to moderate opposition. But it lagged in its western axis of advance, which proved critical because Clark's Fifth Army was to land at Salerno, south of Naples, and needed Montgomery's troops to make contact before the Germans could reinforce their defenses in that area.

On September 9 Operation Avalanche, the amphibious assault at Salerno, was launched by Major General Ernest J. Dawley's U.S. VI Corps and Major General Richard L. McCreery's British X Corps, both part of Clark's Fifth Army. Kesselring's forces responded rapidly and savagely. German reinforcements poured into the area at unbelievable speed; their intense fire kept the Allied troops pinned down in a small beachhead. On the darkest day, September 16, six enemy divisions simultaneously struck the Allied lines. At several points the Germans penetrated almost to the sea, but after frightening losses on both sides they were pushed back.

The Salerno beachhead was finally secured on September 18, though Allied troops were unable to move inland. Montgomery's Eighth Army had established contact with the Salerno force on the 16th, and Kesselring had begun a gradual, orderly pullback of his forces in the Salerno area that same day. On the 20th Clark visited the Salerno beachhead, decided Dawley was not sufficiently aggressive, and replaced him with Major General John P. Lucas as leader of the VI Corps. Clark was in an awkward position regarding both officers—they were good friends of Chief of Staff Marshall and were older than Clark. Allied casualties at Salerno were more than fifteen thousand. Fierce fighting there had demonstrated the awesome skill of the Germans in defensive warfare and proved to be a harbinger of rough times for the Allies in Italy.

German resistance continued to be resourceful and stubborn as Clark's Fifth Army pushed up the west side of the Italian peninsula while Montgomery's Eighth Army advanced on the Americans' east flank. The rugged backbone of the peninsula was the Apennine Mountains, which provided superb defensive possibilities for Kesselring's defenders. The Americans and British would have preferred advancing along the coastal plains beside the Adriatic Sea on the east and the Tyrrhenian Sea on the west. In many places, however, these coastal stretches were narrow, cut by innumerable streams, and under enemy observation from higher inland positions. Generally the Allied forces were left with the unimaginative recourse of pushing northward ridge by ridge.

Montgomery's seizure of Foggia had provided an important opportunity to get Allied air power into action quickly, not only in support of the troops in Italy but also in carrying out strategic bombing runs in Central and Eastern Europe. Likewise, Clark's capture of Naples on October 2 was significant in giving the Allies a major port from which to supply their forces in Italy. For a while, however, the tonnage of Allied sea cargo passing through Naples to Allied forces in Italy was restricted by the necessity to rehabilitate port facilities, railroads, and highways, and by the tremendous amount of materiel that was needed for the quick buildup of the Foggia air complex.

In October, Kesselring, a former head of the Luftwaffe who had now distinguished himself as a master of defense and delay in ground operations, was given overall command of German forces in Italy. Rommel had been in charge in North Italy; he was now transferred to Western Europe.

Kesselring determined to halt the Allies south of Rome at least through the coming winter by establishing several cleverly designed defensive lines in front of both the Fifth and Eighth armies.

On Clark's front, the Germans' first stand was along the Volturno River, about forty miles north of Naples. On October 12, with McCreery's X Corps on the left and Lucas's VI Corps on the right, the Fifth Army began crossing the Volturno in spite of strong German resistance. Days of intense fighting followed in mountainous terrain amid torrential rains. The Germans yielded ground slowly and inflicted heavy casualties. An interesting outfit of Clark's army that distinguished itself in the Volturno fighting was the One Hundredth Battalion of the Thirty-fourth Infantry Regiment, which consisted of Japanese Americans from Hawaii. The Eighth Army, to the east of the Fifth Army, had faced similar tough going. Alexander, realizing the exhausted state of his two armies, halted them on November 15 for a short period of rest and regrouping.

When they resumed their offensives the following week, both the Fifth and Eighth armies encountered stronger German defenses than they had previously met: first the Winter Line and then the Gustav Line, both stretching across the peninsula's entire width. On Clark's side, General Heinrich von Vietinghoff's Tenth Army was entrenched in excellent positions in the mountains inland from the Gulf of Gaeta. The Germans had superb fields of fire to cover the valleys of the fast-moving streams that wound between the mountains to the gulf, particularly the Garigliano, Rapido, and Liri rivers. The entrance to the Liri Valley and the principal highway to Rome were guarded by German guns cunningly placed on the mountain above, which featured an ancient Benedictine monastery called Monte Cassino. Clark's troops fought hard to get past this bottleneck but were stopped near the Rapido, a powerful mountain river several miles southeast of Cassino.

Through November and December 1943 the Fifth Army

struggled to maintain morale and combat effectiveness while confronting superior German forces ensconced in almost impregnable positions. Weather conditions were often impossible, changing from freezing rain to snow and sometimes blizzards. Kesselring was outstanding at shifting his mobile reserves from one front to the other; his job was made easier by Alexander's inexplicable alternating of the Fifth and Eighth armies' major attacks.

The impact of preparations for Overlord was debilitating for Allied operations in Italy. In December 1943 the vast majority of American men and materiel shipped to the European war went to Bolero, the buildup in the British Isles for the cross-channel invasion. In addition, American units and commanders were being transferred from Italy, Sicily, and Northwest Africa to Britain.

The transfer of Allied divisions out of Italy must have been especially depressing to those officers and men left behind. In mid-September the Allies had thirteen divisions in Italy against the Germans' sixteen. By December only eleven Allied divisions remained while Kesselring now had twenty-five. The redeployment of Anglo-American units brought in filler outfits from a wide range of lesser Allied nations, giving both the Fifth and Eighth armies an international flavor, though numerically most were from British Commonwealth countries. With the Germans usually in well-entrenched defenses and the Allies doing the attacking, it would have been demoralizing for the Allied soldiers to dwell on the old maxim that the attacking force should have five times the strength of the defenders. Neither would it have helped their spirits to know that Stalin scoffed at the idea that Italian operations constituted a second front that drew German divisions away from his front.

That month Eisenhower was chosen as Allied supreme commander for Overlord and shortly set off for England, with British General Henry Maitland "Jumbo" Wilson succeeding him as head of the Mediterranean theater. Montgomery was named head of the British-Canadian XXI Army

Group for Overlord, while Bradley was assigned the American First Army and XII Army Group for the Normandy operations. General Oliver Leese succeeded Montgomery as leader of the British Eighth Army, and Alexander continued over the XV Army Group.

Well before the Allied armies in Italy were stopped by enemy defenses, Churchill's fertile imagination, which often produced unrealistic strategies, was working on a scheme to bypass the Winter and Gustav lines with an amphibious assault at Anzio, which lay on the Tyrrhenian coast sixty miles north of the front lines and thirty miles south of Rome. In rather hasty fashion, the Combined Chiefs and their planners developed Operation Shingle, a plan for the Anzio attack. Clark objected that his army could not penetrate the Winter and Gustav lines soon enough to relieve the Shingle force. He got Eisenhower's backing, so Alexander dropped the plan. Churchill persisted, however, and the operation was revived.

Beginning January 17, 1944, Clark sent his Fifth Army in attacks against the Winter Line, none of which achieved a decisive penetration. The U.S. Thirty-sixth Infantry Division was bloodily repulsed in its attempt to cross the Rapido River, and one of its regiments was wiped out. Lucas's VI Corps had been pulled out of the line for the Shingle Operation; it had been replaced along the Rapido by Keyes's II Corps.

On January 22 the VI Corps assaulted Anzio and, catching Kesselring by surprise for once, met light opposition. But Lucas failed to push his troops inland fast enough to seize the Alban Hills overlooking the beachhead. That lapse proved costly, for Kesselring rushed troops onto the high ground with great speed; two weeks into the landing, seventy thousand Germans faced fifty thousand Anglo-Americans at Anzio. As had been true in numerous earlier battles, Truscott's Third Division was outstanding during the Anzio fighting. The low point for the VI Corps came in the latter half of February when General Hans G. Mackensen's German Fourteenth Army delivered almost daily attacks, pushing the Allies nearly to the sea. On February 23, in the midst of this critical situation, Clark appointed Truscott in Lucas's stead as commander of the VI Corps. Like Dawley at Salerno, Lucas was found wanting in aggressiveness. Under Truscott's superior leadership, the beachhead was saved, but for the next three months the troops could not break out and often were pinned down by heavy enemy fire from the Alban Hills positions and from frequent Luftwaffe raids.

Meanwhile, frantic efforts to break through the German lines and relieve the Anzio force continued. French and New Zealand units were brought in to assist the American efforts, particularly in capturing Monte Cassino. One of the more desperate attempts, based on an erroneous report that the Germans were using the monastery as a fortress, was a 255-bomber raid on February 14 that destroyed the monastery. Once it had been reduced to rubble, the Germans turned the ruins into a defensive position. The Cassino stronghold did not fall to the Allies until May 18. After Hitler's grudging permission to Kesselring to move his forces northward to the Gothic line in North Italy, Fifth Army forces broke through the Winter and Gustav lines, pursuing the withdrawing German Tenth Army and threatening the southern flank of the German Fourteenth Army in the Anzio area.

The breakout from Anzio into the Alban Hills finally took place on May 23. It had taken four months and cost 33,000 Allied casualties, mostly American. Churchill admitted during the operation, "We hoped to land a wild cat that would tear out the bowels of the Boche. Instead we have stranded a vast whale with its tail flopping about in the water."

Instead of moving northeast to the key highway junction at Valmontone to block the escape of both German armies, Clark decided to dispatch his Fifth Army toward Rome. The Germans fled northward to confront the Allies later, while Clark grabbed the headlines leading his troops into Rome on June 4. His publicity gesture, as many of his detractors have called it, was short-lived: two days later came the Normandy invasion. Rarely again would the Italian operations receive much attention in the American press.

Above Rome the American Fifth and British Eighth armies kept the pressure on the retreating Germans. Clark's plans to exploit the situation were thwarted by waning logistical support and the loss of Truscott's VI Corps, which had been withdrawn in order to lead the assault on the French Riviera in Operation Dragoon, beginning August 15. In spite of these handicaps, the Fifth Army captured Florence on August 11.

The rapid advance soon was halted for both Allied armies, however, as they ran into well-fortified German positions in mountainous country along the peninsula-wide Gothic Line. The two Allied armies launched simultaneous offensives on August 25; by the end of September they had broken through the Gothic Line, but at a cost of fifty thousand Allied casualties. Alexander then stopped his armies for resupply and regrouping. During the rest of the autumn and winter the battlefront in North Italy was relatively inactive except for limited advances by the Eighth Army along the Adriatic coast. The extremely rugged terrain across much of the two armies' fronts elsewhere, together with unusually heavy rainfall and later deep snow, restricted operations.

Even though combat slowed, there was movement in the high command. In November, McCreery succeeded Leese as head of the Eighth Army. The next month Alexander became supreme Allied commander in the Mediterranean theater, replacing Wilson, who went to head the British Joint Staff Mission in Washington. In turn, Clark moved up to command the XV Army Group while Truscott took over the Fifth Army.

By the winter of 1944–1945 the prospects for more men and materiel were bleak for the Allies in Italy. The focus of the American Joint Chiefs throughout 1944 had been on Eisenhower's operations in Northwest Europe. Even the war with Japan seemed to be of more importance to the JCS by then, especially Nimitz's Central Pacific drive. It must have been difficult for Alexander, Clark, Truscott, and McCreery—the new high command in Italy—to find much to celebrate in their promotions because the Italian front had become part of the backwaters of the war, of declining military significance to the emerging superpowers, the United States and the Soviet Union. At least Churchill and Brooke, his loyal army chief, retained a proprietary interest in Italy, viewing military developments there as primarily of British concern. By then the Eighth Army occupied about two-thirds of the front line across Italy. No wonder Allied troops in Italy felt as though they were fighting a forgotten campaign during the final half-year of the European war.

By early April 1945 the Allies had the equivalent of nineteen divisions in Italy, compared with twenty-six German divisions. On April 16 Clark ordered his two armies on the offensive in "the final battle for Italy." The Fifth Army took Bologna on April 21, and two days later the two Allied armies reached the Po River. The expected German stand there did not materialize; rather, superior U.S. and British armor and mechanization achieved a large-scale rout, with Germans surrendering by the scores of thousands. Italian regular units attached to the Allied armies, together with Italian guerrilla forces, now were fighting openly against the retreating Germans. The Fifth Army was moving at such a wild pace that it reached Milan on April 29, to find it already secured by partisans, and entered Turin the next day, the German defenders having fled. The Eighth Army made similar rapid advances to the east. On April 30 Clark issued a communiqué stating, "Troops of the XV Army Group have so smashed German Armies in Italy that they have been eliminated as a military force." German forces in Italy, totaling almost one million, surrendered unconditionally on May 2. This marked the first of a series of large-scale

capitulations by German military forces that would culminate
in the surrender of Germany throughout Europe the next
week.

The Italian front had produced no dramatic, decisive
developments in the ultimate defeat of Germany. On the
other hand, it had sapped German ground and air strength
that might have been used against the Overlord invaders or
on the Soviet front. It also helped to damage industry,
transportation, utilities, military facilities, and public morale
in Germany itself. So much attention has been given to the
missions of the Combined Bomber Offensive (Pointblank)
staged from Britain that it should be remembered that some
of the largest and most destructive raids came from Foggia
and numerous other Anglo-American bases in Italy. The
Italian front also forced Hitler to hold divisions in the
Balkans to guard against an Allied invasion from Italy
across the Adriatic Sea. For American troops, service in Italy
must have been frustrating as the priority of the front
steadily declined. In retrospect, however, the ugly war in
Italy played a significant role in Germany's final collapse.

7

The Liberation of France and Belgium

THE SUCCESSFUL MOUNTING of Operation Overlord,
the Normandy invasion that was destined to be the largest
seaborne assault in history, was never taken for granted by
the ever-cautious British chiefs or even by the more enthusiastic American chiefs. To make the cross-channel attack
work, four crucial problems had to be resolved. First, the
campaign against the German U-boats must reach a level of
effectiveness that would secure the lines of communication
between America and Britain and between South England
and Normandy. This had been largely achieved by late 1943.

Second, Operation Pointblank, the Combined Bomber
Offensive, must temporarily concentrate on crippling the
Luftwaffe severely enough to prevent it from interfering
with Overlord, and must destroy road and rail facilities
that would allow German reinforcements to enter the invasion zone. The British and American bomber commands
achieved both these goals well before D-day.

Third, Operation Bolero, the buildup in the British Isles,
must be completed. In an unprecedented logistical feat,
nearly two million American and Canadian personnel were
transported across the Atlantic by late May 1944, along with
huge amounts of equipment ranging from cigarettes to
entire trains. For their part, the British provided a good
portion of the building materials, utilities, new roads, and
countless services needed for the newcomers' bases and
training grounds.

Fourth, and often overlooked by Western historians, Over-lord's success depended heavily upon the fulfillment of Stalin's pledge at Tehran to unleash his mightiest offensive yet on the Eastern Front at the time of the Normandy invasion. This was done on time and kept Hitler from redeploying large forces from the East. So vital was the role of the Soviet offensive that in its absence the Germans would probably have driven the Overlord invaders back into the English Channel.

When Eisenhower arrived in London in January 1944 as supreme Allied commander for Overlord, planning for the invasion was already well advanced. An Anglo-American planning staff, established by the Combined Chiefs of Staff, had been at work for many months under the able direction of British Lieutenant General Frederick E. Morgan. With the coming of Montgomery and Bradley, the two Overlord army group leaders, together with Eisenhower and his principal staff officers from the Mediterranean theater, the invasion planning was accelerated, and many revisions were made before a final plan evolved that spring.

The high command for Overlord was a mixture of skilled and experienced American and British officers who by then had often worked with one another. Although Brooke had hoped for the position, Eisenhower had been named as the supreme commander of the Allied Expeditionary Force, as it was officially designated. The deputy supreme commander was an Eisenhower favorite, Air Chief Marshal Arthur W. Tedder of the Royal Air Force. The Allied naval commander was British Admiral Bertram H. Ramsay, while the air commander was Air Chief Marshal Trafford Leigh-Mallory of the RAF. Eisenhower was also to be the Allied ground commander after he moved his headquarters to Normandy. Until then, all Allied ground forces would be under Montgomery, who also headed the XXI Army Group, con-sisting of Lieutenant General Miles C. Dempsey's British Second Army and Lieutenant General Henry Crerar's Canadian First Army.

The seeds of dissension were sown in the provision that until Eisenhower took overall ground command, that authority lay with Montgomery. This meant that the two American armies, Bradley's First and Patton's Third, would be temporarily under the volatile Monty. Both American army commanders already had strong negative impressions of Montgomery from their Mediterranean associations, and Monty did not think highly of them either, or, in fact, of Eisenhower.

The assaults on D-day were to be conducted on two beaches, designated Omaha and Utah, by three American divisions of the First Army, and on three beaches to the east by two British divisions and one Canadian of the British Second and Canadian First armies. The follow-up forces would be the U.S. Third Army in the American sector and the rest of the Canadian First Army in the British sector. Three airborne divisions, including two American, were to be dropped behind the beaches shortly before the main assaults.

The enormity of the Overlord undertaking, even in its assembly and training stages in Britain, made inevitable a degree of confusion and chaos, including the loss of men in training exercises. It also led to German awareness of the invasion preparations despite efforts at secrecy. Enemy knowledge of the greatly increased military activity in the British Isles proved to be both an asset and a liability for the Allies.

When Patton was brought to England in early 1944, Eisenhower promised him command of the Third Army after it was moved to Normandy as a follow-up force after D-day, but initially Patton was to participate in Operation Fortitude. This was an incredibly successful Anglo-American cover plan to deceive the Germans into believing that the Allies planned a secondary attack on Norway with a non-existent British army staging from Scotland, while the principal assault would be at Pas de Calais, north of Normandy. Patton, who already had a fearsome reputation among German commanders, would supposedly lead the Calais invasion, utilizing the "ghost" American army that he was widely rumored to be training in South England. The deception was elaborate, including dummy tanks and soldiers and phony radio transmissions. Hitler and the German high command in the West were duped amazingly long by Fortitude, not releasing large forces from the Calais area until weeks after D-day.

Whereas German interest in the Fortitude activities proved to be a plus, the enemy's chance discovery of another preinvasion operation in Britain turned out to be disastrous for the Allies. In the early morning darkness of April 28, 1944, nine German torpedo boats on patrol in the English Channel picked up heavy radio traffic in Lyme Bay in South England. Speeding to the area, they discovered a convoy of eight LSTs (Landing Ship, Tank) loaded with American soldiers, who were participating in one of many landing exercises staged that spring. A single Allied warship provided protection for the LSTs and was not even on the same radio frequency with them. The fast German boats took full advantage of the vulnerable troop vessels, sinking two and damaging several others. The official report of the details of the disaster was withheld until 1974. It stated that 749 American soldiers and sailors were killed off Slapton Sands in Lyme Bay that terrible night. Later unofficial researchers claimed the true figure was nearer to 1,000 dead. Ironically, the Fourth Infantry Division, to which most of the troops belonged, would lose about one-fourth as many men at Utah Beach on D-day.

The Normandy invasion of June 6, 1944, is important as the greatest amphibious assault in history and (even to senior German commanders) as the beginning of the end of Hitler's Third Reich. German defenders at the targeted Normandy beaches must have felt awed to observe more than five thousand Allied ships moving into position off the Normandy beaches, unleashing at 2 a.m. horrendous naval gunfire in support of a sky filled with attacking Allied aircraft, and unloading four hours later the first waves of landing craft.

In spite of rough surf and cleverly placed beach obstacles,

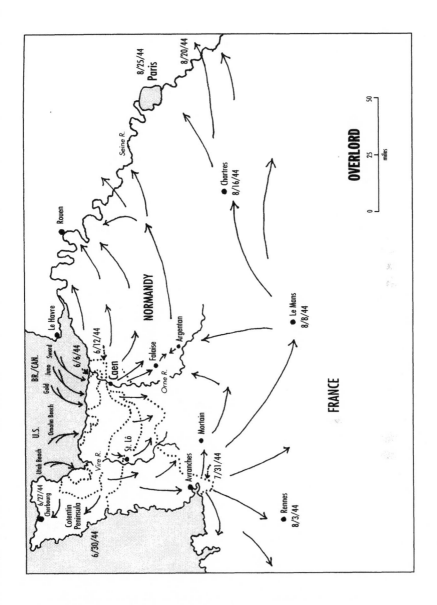

Allied progress on D-day was more favorable than expected on four of their five beaches. Only Omaha Beach developed into a desperate situation, where the American First and Twenty-ninth divisions faced not only rugged bluffs and numerous pillboxes but also greater enemy strength than intelligence had predicted. Before the end of the first day, nevertheless, the Americans at Omaha Beach had secured a firm foothold on the high ground and were beginning to advance inland. American casualties on D-day were 6,500 of the Allied total of 10,500.

Partly because of Fortitude, inclement weather, and Hitler's meddling in defense plans, the German high command, though extremely capable, was slower in responding than the Allies had expected. In overall command in the West was Field Marshal Gerd von Rundstedt; Rommel headed Army Group B, which included the Fifth Panzer Army and the Seventh and Fifteenth armies. Besides this formidable array of firepower in or near the Normandy region, von Rundstedt could call upon German units elsewhere in France and the Lowlands if conditions had been normal—but they were not. Thanks to the French resistance movement and especially to round-the-clock Anglo-American air operations, German ground units found few passable roads, railroads, and bridges into the invasion zone. Where transportation routes were usable, Allied aircraft and partisans made life miserable for enemy reinforcements trying to move on them.

By the end of June about one million Allied soldiers were in the Normandy beachhead, which had been pushed inland but, due to fierce resistance, not far enough to prevent the Germans from shelling almost every sector of the Overlord foothold. During the detailed planning that had preceded the invasion, the focus had been on securing the beachhead rather than advancing into the countryside beyond, because of the Allied leaders' concern that the Germans might repulse the invasion. The result was that Montgomery's and Bradley's officers and men had to improvise and adjust quickly to survive in the Normandy hedgerow (*bocage*) country. The difficulty of the terrain had been underestimated, and the Germans fought with tenacity and cunning for every hedgerow-bordered field. The most savage fighting took place on the British front where German armor remained successful for weeks in defending Caen, one of

Montgomery's prime objectives. On the American front too the effort to break out of the beachhead was stopped, and Bradley was unable to seize quickly one of his main objectives, Saint Lô. While the Germans held firm between Caen and Saint Lô, a thrust out of the beachhead succeeded on the west end when Major General J. Lawton Collins's VII Corps advanced up the Cotentin Peninsula and captured the port of Cherbourg on June 27. The prize proved disappointing, however, because the Germans had so effectively wrecked the harbor and port facilities that they could not handle the huge amount of cargo needed by the Overlord forces. For a long while the forces had to continue relying on artificial harbors ("mulberries") and makeshift over-the-beach arrangements along the Normandy coast.

Preceded by a "carpet bombing" by American heavy and medium bombers of virtually every square yard of the German positions around Saint Lô, Bradley's First Army finally broke out of the beachhead in that area on July 25. At the base of the Cotentin Peninsula, the First Army turned eastward. On August 1 Patton led his Third Army through the opening and sent one corps into the Brittany Peninsula toward Brest; he deployed the rest of his forces southeastward to trap the Germans, now retreating en masse from their Normandy defenses.

With the Third Army's arrival, Bradley became commander of the American XII Army Group, and Lieutenant General Courtney H. Hodges took over the First Army. Meanwhile, Crerar's entire Canadian First Army had reached Normandy, and Montgomery's XXI Army Group now had its basic units, though Monty would continue to be acting head of all Overlord ground forces for another five weeks.

The fast-deteriorating situation for the Germans led to hasty moves by each side. The enemy tried a frantic counterattack in early August toward Avranches, south of Saint Lô, aiming to break through to the sea and cut off the main lines of communication of the American armies. The thrust was stopped in a vicious five-day battle at Mortain, northeast of Avranches, by two First Army divisions fighting against much larger German forces. In mid-August, Canadian and American forces ambitiously tried to encircle a large number of withdrawing Germans east of Avranches. More than sixty thousand enemy soldiers were killed or taken prisoner in the huge trap, and large amounts of artillery, armor, and other vehicles were captured. But many of the fleeing Germans escaped eastward because of a Canadian-American mixup in closing a gap between Falaise and Argentan.

The Third Army left the mop-up in the pocket to the Canadians and Hodges's troops, while Patton pushed his troops northeast toward the Seine. His dash succeeded in preventing the Germans from setting up a defense line along the Seine and led to another large-scale envelopment of enemy forces. In a bold move, Patton relied on an American Ninth Air Force tactical wing to serve as his right flank through much of this lightning advance.

On August 25 occurred the dramatic climax of the Normandy invasion when Major General Leonard T. "Gee" Gerow's V Corps of the U.S. First Army liberated Paris, with a French armored division allowed to lead the way into the French capital. Two days earlier Paris resistance fighters had begun an uprising that compelled the First Army to send in troops to assist. By the time the city fell, elements of the four Allied armies had reached the banks of the Seine west of Paris.

In terms of casualties and destroyed war materiel, the Normandy campaign must be ranked as very costly for both sides. For the Germans it was especially draining because, unlike the Allies, they were unable to replace their enormous losses in men and equipment. Altogether, 637,000 Allied and German casualties occurred during the eighty-five-day campaign, June 6 to August 29, 1944: 400,000 German, 140,000 American, and 97,000 British and other Allied personnel.

By the end of August the German high command in France and the Lowlands had undergone several changes. In

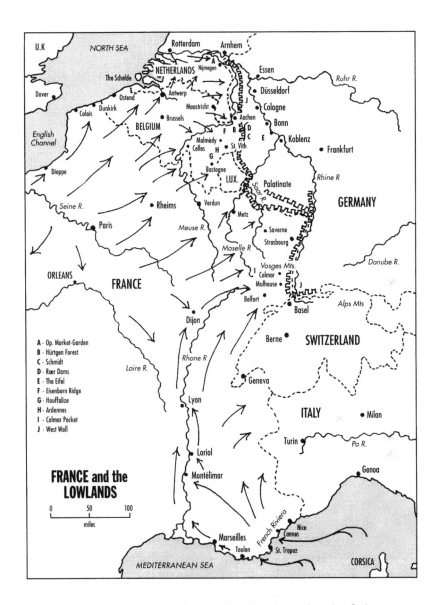

FRANCE and the LOWLANDS

0   50   100

miles

A - Op. Market-Garden
B - Hürtgen Forest
C - Schmidt
D - Roer Dams
E - The Eifel
F - Eisenborn Ridge
G - Houffalize
H - Ardennes
I - Colmar Pocket
J - West Wall

early July Hitler dismissed von Rundstedt as head of the
Western High Command and named Field Marshal Gunther
von Kluge to the post. Two weeks later Rommel was
wounded and replaced by General Walther Model as head of
Army Group B. After heavy German losses in the Falaise-

Argentan pocket, Hitler dismissed von Kluge, who then committed suicide; Model succeeded him. With such command chaos, it is amazing that the Germans conducted so orderly a withdrawal to their defensive positions in West Germany.

It is impressive, too, how tenaciously the Germans fought to hold the French ports below Normandy, particularly along the Bay of Biscay where many of their submarine bases were located. American troops seized Brest in mid-September after a bloody siege, but Saint Nazaire and several other key Biscay ports were denied to the Allies for many months, and German garrisons in some locations along the Bay of Biscay did not capitulate until hostilities ended.

Lacking access to a major port of entry in North France, Allied supply personnel found it increasingly difficult to maintain the fast-expanding lines of communication to the armies as they moved away from Normandy. In a decision that was resented by American ground commanders, especially Bradley and Patton, Eisenhower temporarily assigned top priority on supplies to Montgomery's XXI Army Group. Two considerations dictated his decision: the needs to seize the large port of Antwerp and to overrun German launch sites for V-1 missiles and V-2 rockets, which were bombarding South England.

With the Canadian First Army advancing swiftly along the coast and the British Second Army keeping pace on its east flank, the XXI Army Group swept from the Seine well into Belgium in one week. Montgomery's forces took Brussels on September 3 and Antwerp the following day, but strong German forces did not yield the Schelde, a critical estuary between the sea and Antwerp which had to be secured before the Allies could exploit the port.

In the meantime, while the XXI Army Group raced into Belgium, Bradley's XII Army Group was slowed markedly by reduced logistical support, especially gasoline. Patton's wrath was kindled when his tanks ground to a halt for want of fuel just after crossing the Meuse River at the end of August, while Hodges's First Army also was virtually paralyzed by its lack of supplies. Eisenhower finally moved his headquarters to France on September 3 and assumed overall leadership of ground operations, leaving Montgomery with only his army group command. Some thought Monty's monumental vanity would have been placated by Ike's grant of the supply priority and by Brooke's promotion of him to field marshal. But Monty began a gradually intensifying harassment campaign against Eisenhower, brazenly complaining of his need for more logistical support and criticizing the supreme commander's strategy of a broad-front advance into Germany. Both Brooke and Montgomery believed the stress should be on a single narrow thrust by the XXI Army Group across the relatively flat terrain of the Netherlands and Northwest Germany, climaxed by the capture of Berlin before Soviet forces could get there.

While Monty's eye was on a glorious dash deep into Germany, Eisenhower had to remind the new field marshal that for the time being his main job was to clear Antwerp and thus open the great port for sea cargo in support of both Allied army groups. The Schelde estuary defenses proved hard to crack, however, because they had been cleverly designed and heavily reinforced, including by early September both the German Fifteenth and First Parachute armies.

Meanwhile, Hitler had reassigned von Rundstedt as head of the Western High Command. Although von Rundstedt acknowledged the need to prevent Allied use of the port of Antwerp as long as possible, he was unable further to reinforce the Schelde because Allied forces isolated the area. He wisely decided to strengthen his fortifications along the German border from Switzerland to the sea near Ostend, Belgium, known as the West Wall. His task of revitalizing the shattered remnants of the German army that had retreated across North France was formidable, but von Rundstedt and his senior officers somehow managed to keep their staff and line organizations effective and their troops disciplined. Ahead of the West Wall defenders, however, loomed an advancing Western Allied force that by mid-September totaled more than two million soldiers and included an enormous array of firepower in armor, artillery, and aircraft. Some American and British newspapers were already anticipating the surrender of Germany by Christmas of 1944, but von Rundstedt's forces along the West Wall had plenty of fight left in them.

While the Normandy breakout had been gathering momentum, a new Allied front had been opened in South France. Operation Dragoon (at first code-named Anvil) had been controversial from its earliest planning stages, with Churchill and the British chiefs decrying the drain it would cause on Allied strength in Italy. The ultimate lineup included no major British forces, and the assault finally won British acquiescence, though Churchill grumbled that he had been "dragooned" into accepting it. The main aims of Dragoon were to protect the southern flank of the Overlord invaders, to open another major port for the huge advance into Germany by liberating Marseilles, and ultimately to provide the southernmost army group in the broad-front advance to and beyond the Rhine River.

The invasion began on August 15 along the French Riviera with assaults first by Truscott's VI Corps from Italy and then by General Jean de Lattre de Tassigny's French II Corps. They constituted the reorganized U.S. Seventh Army, now headed by Lieutenant General Alexander M. "Sandy" Patch, a veteran of the Solomons campaign in the South Pacific. Ultra communications intelligence provided superb information about German defenses and movements in the planning and operational phases. On the first day Allied casualties were fewer than two hundred, so light was the German resistance.

The French struck westward along the coast toward Toulon and Marseilles, which they captured after hard battles during the next thirteen days. Meanwhile, the American VI Corps advanced rapidly north of the Riviera against only scattered opposition. The principal German force was General Friedrich Wiese's Nineteenth Army, made up of one good panzer division and seven mediocre infantry divisions. The Germans, other than the garrisons in Toulon and Marseilles, did not seem prepared to fight and fell back in disorder, apparently trying to escape up the Rhone Valley.

Truscott sent a column of his VI Corps to Montélimar to cut off the enemy retreat northward along the Rhone. Unfortunately the fast-moving American column had not enough strength to take the city immediately; it was defended by Wiese's one strong division. Montélimar was captured on August 28 after five days of fighting, but by then much of the German Nineteenth Army had escaped northward along the west bank of the Rhone. Truscott quickly set another trap in the Rhone Valley between Montélimar and Loriol. This time the reinforced Americans took a large toll of the fleeing Germans, including more than fifteen thousand prisoners. By the end of August the Dragoon invaders had badly hurt the German Nineteenth Army, killing or capturing many of its troops, destroying many of its tanks and much of its artillery and other equipment, and forcing the rest of its soldiers to retreat northeast to the Vosges Mountains near the German border.

During the first two weeks of September the Dragoon campaign was completed in good order against minor resistance. On September 11 Truscott's men made contact with Patton's troops near Dijon. Four days later the American-French VI Army Group was established under Lieutenant General Jacob M. Devers. It comprised Patch's American Seventh Army and de Lattre's French First Army. The long Allied line of army groups for the push into Germany was now complete.

8

The West Wall and the Bulge

By September 1944 Devers's VI Army Group on the southern end and Bradley's XII Army Group in the middle of the Allied line each faced logistical shortages and tightening enemy resistance. Montgomery's XXI Army Group confronted some of von Rundstedt's strongest defensive positions as well as a complicated network of canals and rivers in the Lowlands, impeding its advance to the West Wall. In early September, Montgomery persuaded Eisenhower to approve his plan to mount a combined airborne-ground operation toward Arnhem, which lay on the Rhine River in the eastern Netherlands. The British field marshal argued that the offensive would produce a quick Rhine bridgehead and break through the West Wall. He convinced Ike that the operation would be worth delaying the conquest of the Schelde.

The dual action was named Operation Market-Garden, with its airborne phase code-named Operation Market and the ground stage Garden. Although they were permitted little input into the planning, two Americans were the senior airborne officers: Lieutenant General Lewis H. Brereton, who had been MacArthur's air chief in the Philippines at the beginning of the war and who now commanded the newly formed First Allied Airborne Army, made up of two American divisions and one British; and Lieutenant General Matthew B. Ridgway, head of the American XVIII Airborne

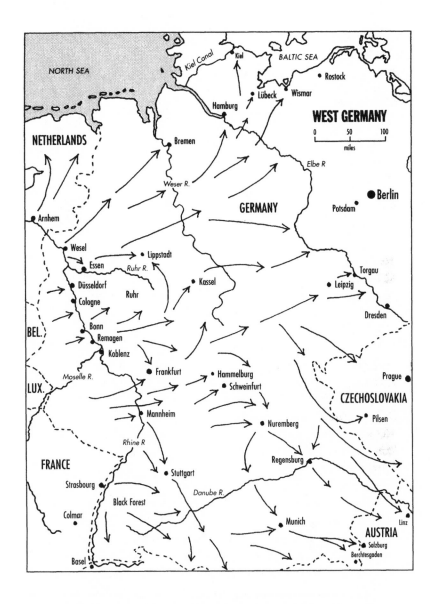

Corps, which consisted of the participating 82nd and 101st divisions. Lieutenant General Brian G. Horrocks would lead the British XXX Corps in an unrealistically conceived drive to Arnhem—over sixty miles along a narrow road across seven key bridges (to be seized by the American paratroopers), with flood plains on either side of the corridor and during a season of normally heavy rains in that region. The British First Airborne Division, meanwhile, would be dropped only seven miles west of Arnhem, to be reinforced shortly by Horrocks's corps after the British paratroopers had seized the vital Rhine bridge at Arnhem.

Almost nothing went as planned for the Allied forces. Market-Garden began on September 17 with the landings of all three airborne divisions and Horrocks's corps beginning its drive toward Arnhem. The American divisions were unable to seize all the bridges on the route of the XXX Corps. The British troops were slowed also by Horrocks's cautiousness in pushing the advance and by German opposition along the restricted corridor of maneuver.

General Kurt Student, commander of the German First Parachute Army, and Field Marshal Model, head of Army Group B, both happened to be in the vicinity, together with a larger number of strong German units than Allied intelligence had indicated. The two senior German commanders quickly ordered reinforcements into the Arnhem area and launched powerful counterattacks. The British corps was unable to reach the British airborne troops near Arnhem. This resulted in superior enemy firepower decimating the paratroopers' ranks and led to the surrender of some of the remnants and the desperate flight of the rest from the Arnhem vicinity in late October. The American airborne forces fought on despite severe losses until they were ordered to pull back on November 6, by which time the Allied high command had admitted Market-Garden to be a failure. "Poor weather [preventing the full use of Allied air power], the inability of the British Second Army to move north rapidly or to widen the corridor, Allied failure to concentrate enough strength at Arnhem, and the rapid German reaction spelled its [Market-Garden's] doom," concludes an authority.

Disappointed but undeterred in his determination to lead the way into Germany, Montgomery now concentrated on what should have been his first order of business all along, namely, the reduction of the Schelde defenses and the opening of the port of Antwerp. Ultimately it took the concerted efforts of not only large elements of the British and Canadian armies but also the help of the American First Army to clear the Schelde estuary of Germans. The fighting finally ended November 8, but the port could not be opened until the end of that month when the last German mines were swept from the ship channel to Antwerp.

The Market-Garden disaster and the Schelde operations left Montgomery unable to spearhead the attack into Germany for some time, so Eisenhower designated Bradley's army group to receive priority logistical support in October in preparation for a major move across the Rhine. Lieutenant General William H. Simpson's U.S. Ninth Army was added that month to the XII Army Group's lineup against the West Wall. The Ninth and First armies, backed by massive close air support from the Ninth Air Force, opened an offensive toward the Rhine in mid-November. Assigned a sector of the front between the U.S. First Army to the south and the British Second Army to the north, Simpson's troops quickly ran into strong enemy positions and at first made slow progress. In the sector of the First Army the American soldiers, mainly of the V Corps, collided with potent German defenses in the dense Hürtgen Forest, where the fiercest fighting yet along the West Wall developed. In his attempts to seize the Roer River dams on the far edge of the Hürtgen Forest near Schmidt, General Hodges was forced to commit more and more of his First Army units to the growing bloodbath.

The Third Army, meanwhile, had rammed into a powerful ring of fortresses around Metz that turned Patton's former dash into a costly stalemate. Not until mid-December, nearly a month after his fight to seize Metz had begun, was the final fortress captured. Other elements of his army, on the other hand, had continued to advance, establishing bridgeheads across the Saar River by the time the Metz area was secured. Harsh winter weather handicapped Patton as he prepared to drive into South Germany.

For unknown reasons, Devers and his VI Army Group have been largely forgotten in accounts of the war against Germany. During the autumn of 1944, however, the longest advances by the Western Allies in Europe were made by Devers's forces. Patch's Seventh Army, on Patton's right flank, pushed into the Vosges Mountains and captured Strasbourg on the west side of the Rhine on November 23, holding it against several strong enemy counterattacks. Farther south in the Vosges, de Lattre's French First Army took Mulhouse and reached the banks of the Rhine not far north of the Swiss border. The Germans clung to a large pocket around Colmar in the Vosges region as severe winter conditions set in, restricting operations in the rough terrain. Amazingly, the German Nineteenth Army, which had been severely crippled in the Dragoon campaign, had been reorganized and provided with reinforcements and more weapons; it now fought fiercely against the French in the Colmar pocket.

Except for some surprising gains by Devers's troops, Allied progress toward Germany had been somewhat disappointing in October and November 1944, especially in contrast to the race across North France. On the other hand, the logistical picture had improved markedly by early December. The ports of Antwerp and Brussels, as well as Cherbourg to a lesser degree, were handling incoming cargoes at near maximum capacity. A large, well-operated communications organization, with headquarters in Paris, now was functioning well in support of American and French forces, with well-stocked supply and ordnance depots behind the armies and improved road and rail lines to the front. Eisenhower's headquarters and that of Spaatz's U.S. Strategic Air Command also had moved to Paris. At last it seemed that logistically and administratively the long line of Allied armies had the wherewithal to launch their offensives across the Rhine into Germany.

At a conference in Maastricht in eastern Belgium on December 7, Eisenhower personally informed Bradley and

Montgomery that he expected them to get their army groups on the attack soon. Montgomery's forces were to conduct the primary offensive north of the Ruhr Valley industrial region of western Germany, which seemed better suited for mobile warfare than the rough country in the paths of the American army groups to the south. Bradley's army group was to undertake secondary offensives against the West Wall from Aachen through the Hürtgen Forest to the Saar region.

During the meeting at Maastricht, says Eisenhower's chief biographer, "The relationship between Eisenhower and Montgomery seemed to have reached a breaking point, but neither of the two men was willing to carry things to that extreme." Monty had objected to Eisenhower's belief that Patton's armored forces should be allowed to make a strong thrust through the plains between Frankfurt and Kassel, inside Germany. He had also been irritated by Ike's refusal to give him command of all operations above the Ardennes in eastern Belgium. The whole argument must have puzzled Bradley, for it seemed that Eisenhower was again giving the British XXI Army Group priority, though the supreme commander reiterated that he was not basically abandoning his broad-front strategy. Ike claimed he was merely giving Monty's forces the primary offensive for the push beyond the Rhine and past the Ruhr.

The main effect of Eisenhower's latest strategic turn was to push Montgomery and Bradley to prepare offensives, which they quickly did upon returning to their headquarters. With Devers's troops also rolling into action again soon, the whole Western Front was expected to be active by January 1945, with Allied armies on the attack. The only exception was in the Ardennes area where Major General Troy H. Middleton's VIII Corps was spread out in a very thin cordon defense in the middle of the First Army's sector.

Hitler had also been contemplating offensive action for that period of the winter; it would be concentrated against the Americans in the Ardennes. Eisenhower and his senior commanders had discounted the probability of their offensive plans being disrupted by a preemptive German assault. They figured the much-respected von Rundstedt would not risk his main forces, including his sparse reserves, in such an unwise gamble; but Hitler, overriding the counsel of von Rundstedt and other high-ranking officers, decreed that his Ardennes plan be implemented, whatever the cost.

Hitler believed that a decisive victory in the Ardennes would deprive the Allies of Antwerp, isolate the British XXI Army Group, and make the Western Allies amenable to a negotiated peace on terms favorable to Germany. Then he could turn all his forces against the Soviets and crush them. By then Hitler had virtually withdrawn into a world of his own, totally separated from reality. Von Rundstedt later commented, "The available forces were far too small for such an ambitious plan. It was a nonsensical operation, and the most stupid part of it was the setting of Antwerp as the target." But the Führer would not listen to his top generals and compromised only to the extent of postponing the assault from November 25 to December 16.

The forces Hitler committed to his Ardennes offensive were considerable. The principal assault units were to be General Josef "Sepp" Dietrich's Sixth SS Panzer Army on the north and General Hasso von Manteuffel's Fifth Panzer Army to the south. Supporting efforts would be made by General Gustav von Zangen's Fifteenth Army above Dietrich's army, and General Erich Brandenberger's Seventh Army below von Manteuffel's troops. Short on air support, Hitler would depend on surprise and on expected snowy weather that would curtail Allied air operations during the critical early stages of the offensive.

The Führer moved his headquarters from East Prussia to the Rhineland to take charge personally of Operation Autumn Fog, the code-name for his Ardennes offensive. He hoped to confuse and paralyze the American corps in the initial assault by dropping paratroopers behind the lines to seize key road junctions and by deploying Colonel Otto Skorzeny's special force to infiltrate the American rear, capture the

Meuse bridges, and disrupt road movements. Skorzeny's men were English-speaking, wore American uniforms, and used American vehicles. Although colorful and daring, neither of these schemes that delighted Hitler was especially effective.

Most of the First Army's senior officers and even Eisenhower's intelligence staff were caught by surprise when the Germans attacked in the Ardennes on December 16. Intelligence had shown a buildup of enemy activity across the Rhine in the Eifel region opposite the Ardennes, but the Germans were not using many radio transmissions, thus limiting the data picked up by Ultra. The accelerating enemy movements seemed to indicate an impending limited attack against American positions in the Hürtgen Forest, which adjoined the Ardennes on the north. Middleton's soldiers were quite surprised by the German artillery bombardment of two thousand guns that erupted at 5:35 a.m. on the 16th. The rapid movement of the first waves of enemy panzers and infantry through the VIII Corps's front attested to excellent German preparations and incredibly high esprit de corps.

Von Manteuffel's Fifth Panzer Army viciously sliced through two American divisions and was not stopped until its forward elements had reached Celles, two miles from the Meuse River. Dietrich's Sixth SS Army was slowed by American resistance on the Eisenborn Ridge and at Saint Vith. Von Manteuffel's dramatic advance halted by December 26 because of increasingly strong First Army resistance in the Meuse Valley and the stubborn opposition of American forces at Houffalize and especially Bastogne. These troops had been surrounded and bypassed over sixty miles eastward from the Fifth Panzer's maximum penetration toward the Meuse. Neither of the supporting German armies had gotten much momentum before their advances were checked by belated but effective American defensive actions. In effect, both von Zangen's army to the north and Brandenberger's to the south barely gained footholds on the west side of the

Saar River and were never of much assistance to the two main assault armies.

The American defense of Bastogne included elements of several units, but the nucleus was the 101st Airborne Division. The Bastogne defenders held out for more than a week against superior German forces, who were astounded by the reply to their surrender ultimatum by the 101st's acting commander, Brigadier General Anthony McAuliffe: "Nuts!" The Americans were relieved on December 26 by Patton's Third Army, a portion of which he personally led in a sudden ninety-degree turn northward from their planned Saar offensive to rush 150 miles through heavy snows to lift the siege of Bastogne. Once again Patton had vindicated Eisenhower's decision to keep him as an army commander. The American garrison at Saint Vith, after being a thorn in the side of Dietrich's army for almost a week, was driven out by the Germans on December 21.

Desperate Germans had earlier committed isolated atrocities against American troops, but the worst yet occurred on December 16–18 when Colonel Jochen Peiper led his armored unit of the First SS Panzer Division into the Malmédy area and massacred troops and civilians at several locations. The largest number of atrocities occurred at Malmédy on the 17th when an American unit surrendered to Peiper's superior force. The 120 GIs were lined up in a field and machine-gunned by two tanks. A dozen Americans who escaped were trapped in a building in the town; the Germans set it afire and then shot to death all the men as they were forced out by the smoke and flames. All told, Peiper's unit murdered 308 American troops and 111 French civilians, according to the official report, though later researchers estimate the real figures were about double those numbers. Peiper was tried after the war and received the death sentence; it was then commuted to a prison term, and after seven years in jail he was freed.

While Hitler was turning down von Rundstedt's requests for various realignments of his forces to cope with the unexpected American holdouts at Bastogne and elsewhere, Eisenhower met with Bradley, Montgomery, and their army commanders at Verdun, France, on December 19. The atmosphere was subdued at first in view of the huge bulge the Germans had already punched in the Ardennes region. The supreme commander, however, had called the session to plan the elimination of the salient. He began confidently: "The present situation is to be regarded as one of opportunity for us and not disaster. There will be only cheerful faces at this conference table." Ike decided the campaign could be prosecuted more effectively if Montgomery were given temporary command of the northern half of the salient line and Bradley the southern half. In fact, all U.S. forces above the Ardennes were placed temporarily under Monty. These included all of Simpson's Ninth Army and two of the key corps of Hodges's First Army—Collins's VII and Ridgway's XVIII Airborne corps (the latter deployed as elite infantry in this campaign). Not surprisingly, Bradley was disgruntled, but he cooperated well, especially since two of Patton's Third Army corps were on the way to the south side of the salient.

With the weather clearing and the quick and devastating response of Allied airpower against the Germans, enemy casualties began to mount fast. German armor was running desperately short of fuel. And Hitler only slowly allowed von Rundstedt to withdraw units from the now-doomed salient. Montgomery and Bradley launched offensives against the northern and southern walls of the salient on January 3, and by the 16th the Battle of the Bulge was over, with the Germans having retreated eastward back across the Rhine. To Bradley's relief, he got control of the U.S. First Army again two days later, but the American Ninth Army remained under Montgomery's command.

American casualties were 81,000 of the Allied total of 83,000, while the Germans incurred more than 100,000 casualties. American and German forces both lost heavily in artillery, armor, planes, and other equipment. As with the Normandy losses, the ultimate consequences of the enormous

Bastogne campaign were felt more dearly by the Germans, who would not be able to replace the men and materiel lost in Hitler's megalomaniac gamble of perhaps his best armies on the Western Front.

Unhappily, it cannot be said that the senior American army officers involved in the operation were much disposed to celebrate after the Ardennes triumph. For one thing, Patton had argued strongly that deep penetration by armored units across the base of the salient could trap the two German armies that had spearheaded the offensive toward the Meuse. Bradley and Montgomery, however, were more cautious and decided to reduce the Bulge from the Celles area at the western tip, gradually forcing the Germans eastward across the Rhine. This unimaginative approach was denounced by American armored leaders then and ever since because it enabled the bulk of the remaining German attackers to escape in an orderly withdrawal. More disturbing to Patton and his fellow armor enthusiasts, it revealed that even at this late stage in the war, army officers above them did not yet appreciate the devastating power of tank forces. Armor could have caused major disruptions and disarray in the enemy's rear in an opportune situation like the final phase of the Ardennes campaign.

For another thing, to Bradley's consternation, Montgomery had persuaded Ike to let him keep the U.S. Ninth Army as he advanced north of the Ruhr. In addition, Monty had upset all the Americans involved in the Battle of the Bulge, especially Bradley, Hodges, and Patton, by proclaiming at a press conference on January 7 that he had thrown "the whole available power of the British Group of Armies... [into the Ardennes battle] with a bang" and had saved the American First Army from its predicament. In truth there had been only minute British troop participation in the Battle of the Bulge, and British casualties were fewer than two thousand. It was not at all hard for the American commanders to dislike Montgomery. Anglo-American relations temporarily soured in the aftermath of this grand victory.

9

From the Rhine to the Elbe

As ALLIED FORCES encountered enemy defenders along the West Wall and identified the opposing units, they were surprised at how many of the German armies, corps, and divisions bore the same names as those that had been supposedly wrecked as effective fighting outfits in Normandy or the Schelde. When the year 1945 began, the Germans continued to display impressive skill in revitalizing forces, developing clever defensive positions, fighting fiercely, and withdrawing in orderly fashion to the next lines eastward. They also demonstrated a capacity to mount surprise counterattacks—not only in the Ardennes.

In addition to Operation Autumn Fog in eastern Belgium, Hitler also conceived an unrealistic plan for an offensive through the Saverne Gap of the Vosges Mountains, northwest of Strasbourg, France, in the VI Army Group's sector. By planning the assault to begin on January 1, the Führer hoped it would force Eisenhower to shift units from the Ardennes to the Saverne-Strasbourg area to assist Patch's Seventh Army. Fortunately for the Americans who were attacked, Devers and Patch had good intelligence about the impending German move, and their troops were dug in and alert. They were lucky, too, that the German units involved in the Saverne offensive were understrength and poorly equipped and supplied.

General Johannes Blaskowitz, head of German Army

Group G, could draw on only part of his First Army, with three corps bearing the burden of the attempted breakthrough to the Saverne Gap and beyond. For ten days or so the Germans made limited progress west of the Rhine; then they were thrown back by the American Seventh Army, supported by elements of de Lattre's French First Army on its south flank. The German counterattack ended on January 26 as several of its participating divisions were transferred east to cope with a new Soviet thrust.

In the aftermath of the Saverne operation, the French First Army finally reduced the Colmar pocket to the south, the battered German Nineteenth Army fleeing across the Rhine into Germany by February 9. By then, all three Allied army groups had reached or were near the Rhine at many points, from the Canadian lines along the North Sea coast to the French above the Swiss border.

The Rhineland conquest fell into three stages, as planned at Eisenhower's headquarters: Montgomery's offensive to the Rhine, followed by Bradley's, and culminating in the crossing of the Rhine, with Monty's forces making the main thrust. It began with a three-week drive in February by the Canadian First, British Second, and American Ninth armies of the XXI Army Group. Despite fierce enemy resistance, the offensive took them to the Rhine banks from the Nijmegen area of the eastern Netherlands on the north to the edge of Cologne, Germany, on the south.

Bradley's XII Army Group attacked at the same time in support of Montgomery's forces, the bitterest fighting taking place in the long-stalemated area around the Roer dams on the eastern edge of the Hürtgen Forest. The dams were not seized until the Germans had opened their discharge valves and flooded the lower reaches of the Roer River, halting the Ninth Army's advance for two weeks. The Canadians and British to the north were slowed also, not only by stubborn German defenses but by heavy rains and flooding streams. Simpson's army managed to cross the swollen Roer on February 28 and pushed on toward the Rhine, with all three of Monty's armies drawing up to the Rhine by March 10.

To the south of Montgomery's offensive, rapidly changing situations along the American armies' fronts led to modifications of their roles in the advance into Germany. Instead of merely supporting Montgomery's thrust, for instance, armored forces of Hodges's First Army were unexpectedly able on March 7 to seize the Rhine bridge at Remagen, the only one left intact along the great river. Quickly First Army troops poured into Germany between Cologne and Koblenz. The Remagen bridge finally collapsed under the heavy use on March 17, by which time a number of pontoon bridges were carrying much of the American traffic in the area.

Farther south, during the latter half of March, Patton's Third Army and Patch's Seventh Army engaged in a well-coordinated campaign in the Palatinate region, southeast of Luxembourg, which resulted in the virtual elimination of the German First and Seventh armies and the end of the enemy's hold on territory west of the Rhine. The Allied advances were too much for Hitler to tolerate: on March 10 he again fired von Rundstedt as supreme commander in the West, appointing Kesselring as his successor.

Allied offensives in the Rhineland had cost the Germans more than 310,000 casualties, including at least 250,000 troops captured. As his commanders well knew, Hitler had missed the opportunity to move his armies across the Rhine before they were severely damaged or destroyed. From the east bank of the Rhine it is probable that the German armies, if preserved in strength, could have stopped the Allied advance for a long while. The reasons for the Führer's insistence that his Western Front commanders make their main stands west of the Rhine has long been debated by historians; like his decision to launch the Ardennes offensive, Hitler's motivation was probably based less on rational than on emotional and psychological factors by that time.

Patton's Third Army had taken 300,000 prisoners from August 1, 1944, to March 1, 1945, far more than any other army. By the war's end the Third had captured nearly a million German soldiers. Eisenhower, despite having had to protect him again after earlier indiscreet public remarks in England, now praised Patton profusely: "You have made your Army a fighting force that is not excelled in effectiveness by any other of equal size in the world"—or, he might have added, in history.

Unfortunately, at the zenith of his military success and popularity, in late March Patton again acted precipitately. Learning that his son-in-law was in a prison camp in Hammelburg, east of Frankfurt, Patton dispatched a small armored command of three hundred men in sixteen tanks, twenty-seven half-tracks, seven jeeps, and three motorized assault guns to hit the prison camp forty miles away, liberate as many prisoners as possible (the camp held about five thousand, including fifteen hundred Americans), and return to Third Army lines. In the melee at the camp, Patton's son-in-law was wounded and others of the strike force were killed, wounded, or captured, including the captain in command. Loaded with as many prisoners as their vehicles could carry, the rescue mission started back but was ambushed by a German unit. Most of the remnants of the American force were killed or captured, with the liberated prisoners being sent back to their prison camp.

Two days later Patch's Seventh Army captured Hammelburg and the camp, where they rescued Patton's son-in-law and moved him and the other wounded to an American hospital. American and British media featured the story as a Pattonesque gesture of reckless bravado, sacrificing American soldiers' lives to save his son-in-law. "How I hate the press," Patton grumbled, though an American general rarely enjoyed more glory in the media.

On March 28 Eisenhower announced to Montgomery and Bradley his plan for the final phase of the war in western Germany. The main focus would be on Bradley's XII Army Group in its drive toward Dresden and Leipzig; there would be no attempt to race the Soviets into Berlin. Montgomery's Canadian and British troops would push northeast through Hamburg to the Baltic coast while Bradley's

American armies, helped now by Simpson's Ninth Army once more, would encircle large German forces in the industrial Ruhr region and continue on to the Elbe where they would meet Soviet forces. At the Yalta Conference in February, FDR, Churchill, Stalin, and their chiefs had agreed on the postwar zones for occupied Germany, so Western Allied troops were not to be expended in a race with the Soviets for territory in Germany. Devers's VI Army Group was to move down the Danube to Linz, Austria, crushing the last organized resistance above Switzerland. His troops also were to eliminate the "National Redoubt," a rumored final-stand defensive works the Germans had created in the German-Austrian Alps; it turned out to be nonexistent.

When he learned of Ike's plan, Montgomery exploded again over Eisenhower's lack of strategy and disregard for postwar implications in containing Soviet expansionism. Neither Eisenhower nor his boss, Marshall, was greatly concerned at the time about objectives that were unrelated to winning the war as quickly as possible. Simpson, head of the Ninth Army, the Western Allied army closest to Berlin at the end of hostilities, remained convinced the rest of his life that his soldiers could and should have captured Berlin. Patton and other senior American officers believed Vienna and Prague should have been taken by American forces. After the war the Soviets would add Prague and all of Czechoslovakia to their Yalta bag of East and Central European spoils. With the wonder of hindsight, it seemed to many Americans as well as the British that their armies should have been allowed to advance farther east in Europe. But the supreme objectives of chief American decision-makers at that time were to preserve American boys and force Germany to capitulate, noble and commonsensical ends by any measure.

The Ruhr area was surrounded by fast-moving American forces of the Ninth and First armies, driving across the northern and southern edges of the region and making contact near Lippstadt on the eastern side on April 1. The

U.S. Fifteenth Army, commanded by General Gerow, was brought into action on the Rhine, or western, edge of the Ruhr pocket. General Model, head of German Army Group B, now found his three armies and another 100,000 troops of miscellaneous other units entrapped in a four-thousand-square-mile area with food and ammunition for only about three weeks but with orders from Hitler to fight to the death. Model disobeyed the Führer's orders to destroy all the Ruhr's extensive manufacturing and communications facilities. Despite the defenders' valiant efforts, including some of the Northwest European war's most intense urban fighting, the superior numbers and firepower of the three American armies enabled them to split the Ruhr pocket by April 14 and four days later to compel the surrender of the remaining German troops. While Model committed suicide, more than 317,000 enemy soldiers in the Ruhr pocket were captured— the largest haul of German prisoners in the war. German Army Group B had fought a ferocious delaying action that kept Bradley from shifting units to the main drive toward the Leipzig-Dresden area.

Meanwhile, to the north on Montgomery's front, the enemy's Army Group H of General Blaskowitz was steadily forced northeastward through the Netherlands by the Canadian First Army, while the British Second Army drove other forces of Blaskowitz back toward the Elbe in the Hamburg area. The British reached the Elbe in late April, took Hamburg on May 3, and seized Lübeck and Wismar near the Baltic Sea just in time to prevent the advancing Soviets from making the turn into the Danish peninsula.

Devers's VI Army Group was pushing during the same period against General Paul Hausser's Army Group G through South Germany and the Danube Valley in Austria. After a hard-fought victory against the Germans defending Nuremberg, Patch's Seventh Army advanced into the Danube Valley and the Austrian Alps. His American forces took Munich on April 30, and four days later elements of Patch's army seized Salzburg and Berchtesgaden. The latter had been Hitler's Alpine retreat and was erroneously thought to have been the focal point of the National Redoubt. By the end of all hostilities a few days later, the U.S. Seventh Army, like Patton's Third, had advance units well past Linz on the Danube in East Austria, with Vienna less than ninety miles to the east. De Lattre's French soldiers, meanwhile, had eliminated enemy resistance in the Black Forest and moved on to the Swiss border and into southwestern Austria.

During the final weeks of war, two American armies encountered ugly situations when French forces tried to seize enemy territories they had not been authorized to take. In South Germany, Patch's Seventh Army had to overcome small but sharp clashes with de Lattre's French First Army over which should occupy the Stuttgart area. Truscott's Fifth Army met trouble with General Alphonse-Pierre Juin's Second Army, which was moving into northwestern Italy. Eisenhower threatened to terminate the French logistical support (largely American) unless they withdrew, which they did grudgingly. The French also proved difficult during the German occupation that followed the war.

On May 5 German forces on Devers's front, mainly Army Force G, capitulated to him, while that same day Montgomery received the surrender of all German forces on the northern end of the Allied line, principally Army Group H, in the Netherlands, Denmark, and Northwest Germany, including garrisons on the coastal islands in the North Sea. By then the situation was growing chaotic for all Allied armies as thousands of German soldiers were fleeing into their lines to escape the advancing Soviets, who were known for their severe treatment of prisoners. A large exodus of civilians in East Europe was also beginning to flood into Allied-occupied territory, most of them displaced persons trying to return home.

On May 7 Admiral Karl Doenitz, head of the German navy and now successor to Hitler, who had taken his own life in a bunker beneath Berlin, represented Germany in the

formal national surrender at Rheims, France, with Lieutenant General Walter Bedell Smith, Eisenhower's chief of
staff, in charge. Stalin insisted on another surrender ceremony in Berlin, which took place the following day, with
British Air Marshal Arthur Tedder representing Eisenhower
and Soviet Marshal Georgi K. Zhukov presiding. In the
United States and Britain, V-E Day was celebrated on May 8,
though the Soviet government's proclamation of Germany's
surrender was not made until May 9.

During the final weeks of fighting, Allied forces from the
North Sea coast to Austria had been facing another logistical
crisis because of the swiftness of their advance on all fronts.
Indeed, some heavy bombers, now lacking strategic targets,
were modified for use as transports. Compounding the
supply shortages was the urgent need to provide for the
unexpectedly huge influx of displaced civilians and German
military personnel fleeing from the Soviets.

Such problems were a harbinger of the complex economic, social, and political obstacles that faced American
and other Allied troops who now had the task of governing
the occupation zones of defeated Germany. Some Americans
would also be required to join British forces in occupying
the northern Adriatic port of Trieste for several years to keep
Italians and Yugoslavs from fighting over it. Still other
unfortunate American ground, sea, and air personnel received orders that their units were shortly being deployed to
the Pacific to participate in the invasion of Japan, expected to
occur in the autumn of 1945. The War and Navy departments in Washington, meanwhile, were busy in the immediate aftermath of the European conflict trying to satisfy as
well as possible the overwhelming demand of the American
public: "Bring Johnny home."

Among the senior American commanders in the war
against Germany, the two most notable who were sent to the
Pacific were Spaatz, to command the strategic bombing
campaign against Japan, and Hodges, to lead his First Army
in the assault on Japan. The most distinguished and disap-

pointed absentee, consigned to heading the Third Army's occupation of Bavaria, was Patton, who had been turned down by MacArthur: "The Pacific is not large enough for both of us," the latter confided to one of his staff generals at his Manila headquarters.

The Western Allied drive deep into Germany confirmed what many escapees from Nazi-occupied Europe had been trying to tell Washington and London for some time—that Hitler's regime was bent on exterminating Jews and other "undesirables" in the worst genocidal program in history. Although the largest and most horrible concentration camps were liberated by the Soviet army, American forces overran a number of these "hell holes," where naked bodies were stacked in high piles and the living were so emaciated that they were near death. Eisenhower himself visited some of the camps and reported back to Marshall: "The things I saw beggar description. The visual evidence and the verbal testimony of starvation, cruelty and bestiality were so overpowering as to leave me a bit sick." Ike made sure that not only German villagers were forced to walk through the camps in their vicinity but also that American congressmen and British members of Parliament saw the horrors on their tours of West Germany.

All told, more than twelve million died in the Nazi concentration camps, including more than six million Jews. The Holocaust, rather than its military campaigns, is likely to be the main memory of the Third Reich a thousand years hence. There is plenty of data to demonstrate that World War II was the deadliest conflict for combatants in military annals, but the fate of Hitler's victims in his concentration camps leaves no question that it was also history's most horrible war for civilians.

PART THREE

The War Against Japan

10

Early Pacific Defeats and Turning Points

BEFORE 1941 Admiral Isoroku Yamamoto, commander of the Japanese Combined Fleet, was a vehement opponent of a war between Japan and the United States. Once his views were overruled, however, he planned the event that catapulted the United States into the war—the attack on Pearl Harbor, Oahu, in December 1941. In targeting Hawaii, he intended not to capture the islands but to destroy the U.S. Pacific Fleet at its home base so that it could not interfere with Japan's conquests in Southeast Asia. There the Japanese high command planned to acquire oil, rubber, and other strategic resources that were essential to support its ongoing war against China. Yamamoto succeeded in temporarily damaging the American capacity to deter Japanese advances, but the Pearl Harbor attack so enraged the American public that full-scale war became inevitable.

Yamamoto's plan provided for a limited carrier raid on American naval and military bases on Oahu. By August 1941 his carrier pilots had begun practicing their movements, and by mid-November the Pearl Harbor Strike Force had assembled in the Kurile Islands, north of the home islands of Japan. Under the leadership of Vice Admiral Chuichi Nagumo, the fleet sailed on November 26, using a northern route to avoid detection. On the morning of December 7, 1941, the Japanese assault began.

Although the American commanders in Hawaii had received general warnings about the possibility of war with Japan, U.S. navy and army units were totally unprepared for battle. The attack on the ships anchored in Pearl Harbor occurred on a Sunday morning, when many officers and men were ashore. The first aircraft concentrated on "Battleship Row," an area where seven battleships were moored. Other planes struck at naval and military installations elsewhere on Oahu, destroying most of the island's combat aircraft on the ground, where they were lined up in order to prevent sabotage. A second wave of planes soon followed. Nagumo decided that a third attack would be too risky and sailed for Japan, unhindered by resistance.

In less than two hours the Japanese had crippled the U.S. Pacific Fleet as well as the air and ground defenses of Oahu. The overwhelming surprise of the attack was reflected in the results: more than 2,400 Americans killed and nearly 1,200 wounded. Most of the deaths occurred on the battleships; the worst damaged, the *Arizona*, was sent to the bottom with most of its 1,400-man crew. Nine naval ships were sunk and 188 planes were destroyed, with many other vessels, aircraft, and military facilities damaged. The Japanese lost only 29 planes, a fleet submarine, and 5 midget submarines. Japanese casualties included 64 dead, plus the crew of the fleet submarine.

Fortunately for the United States, the three American aircraft carriers in the Pacific were not in port at the time of the attack and therefore survived. Also important for the future, the Japanese neglected to destroy the navy yard, repair and maintenance facilities, or fuel reserves at Pearl Harbor, all of which were vital to the American naval effort in the Pacific. In fact, of the ships sunk by the Japanese at Pearl Harbor, some of the battleships were salvaged and later saw action. Several other vessels were also repaired and returned to duty.

The raid on Oahu was not an isolated event in the Japanese operations. Within hours after the Pearl Harbor attack, other Japanese forces began to assault Wake, Guam,

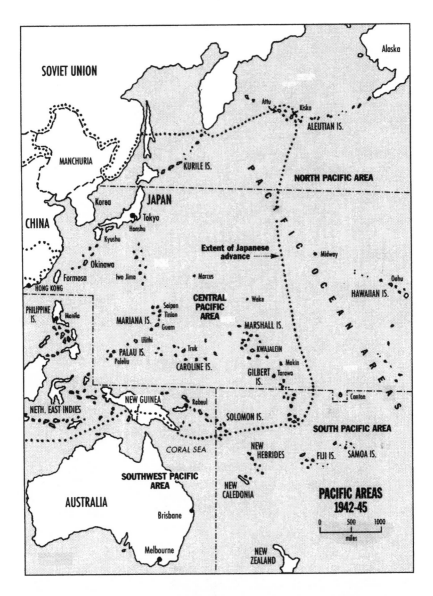

Hong Kong, Malaya, and the Philippines. Surprised Washington analysts had believed the Japanese incapable of executing more than one major offensive at a time. On December 8 President Roosevelt asked Congress to declare war, calling December 7 "a date which will live in infamy." The resolution was passed with one negative vote.

One of the first Allied responses to Japan's wide-ranging attacks was the formation of the American-British-Dutch-Australian Command (ABDACOM), an attempt to defend the Malay Barrier extending from Singapore through the Netherlands East Indies. The United States mainly contributed army aircraft and its small Asiatic Fleet, which had been stationed in the Philippines when the war began. Poorly equipped, vastly outnumbered, and further hampered by command difficulties, ABDACOM struggled from January to March 1942 to hold back Japanese advances along the Malay Barrier. Singapore was lost on February 15. The naval battle of the Java Sea, February 27–March 1, marked one of the final, disastrous defeats in trying to prevent a Japanese invasion of Java. By early March the Japanese held the Netherlands East Indies, and what remained of ABDACOM was dissolved.

The remnants of the participating American forces, largely naval and air, now fled to Australia, which was expected soon to be the target of a Japanese attack. Meanwhile, the Australian government, to Churchill's chagrin, ordered the First Australian Army's main divisions to return home from Egypt where they had been fighting against General Erwin Rommel's Afrika Corps. The Soviet Union, though a potent ally against Germany, would not enter the war against Japan until August 8, 1945.

While the Japanese continued their advances in early 1942, the United States Navy directed a series of limited attacks against Japanese bases in the Pacific. The Pacific Fleet sent out small task forces of cruisers and destroyers, each built around an aircraft carrier, to harass the Japanese outer perimeter in the South and Central Pacific. Under the direction of Admiral Chester Nimitz, the new commander of the Pacific Fleet, raids were launched during February and March against Japanese bases on the Gilbert and Marshall islands, New Britain, Wake, Marcus, and New Guinea, with mixed results.

The most celebrated strike came on April 18, when Tokyo was attacked by sixteen army B-25s, transported to the North Pacific on the carrier *Hornet*. Lieutenant Colonel James H. Doolittle commanded the raid, which caused limited physical damage but had a strong psychological impact, both in the United States and in Japan. The Doolittle mission provided a much-needed boost to American morale, sagging from one Allied defeat after another. In response to the attack, Japanese leaders decided to expand the country's defensive perimeter in order better to protect the home islands. By attempting to do so, they extended their forces beyond their capabilities.

The first targets of the revised Japanese strategy were the southern Solomon Islands and Port Moresby, a strategic Australian base on the south coast of Papua on the island of New Guinea. As the Japanese sent striking forces southward from their strongholds of Truk in the Caroline Islands and Rabaul on the tip of eastern New Britain, the American and Australian navies reacted quickly, informed of the enemy's plans by radio intelligence that had broken the Japanese naval codes. After successfully landing ground troops on Tulagi in the Solomons, the smaller Japanese task force sailed to join the main assault armada for Port Moresby. The opposing naval forces engaged each other in the battle of the Coral Sea on May 7–8. This was the first major carrier battle, one in which the surface ships failed to sight the enemy. In the tactical draw, the Americans and Australians lost more ships and the Japanese more planes. Strategically the Allies won, because the Japanese canceled their plans to capture Port Moresby by sea and withdrew to Rabaul, marking the first time during the war that a Japanese advance was halted. Rear Admiral Frank Jack Fletcher commanded the Allied fleet in the Coral Sea engagement, but he won little praise from Admiral King, who thought he had been too cautious (and had a personality conflict with him).

While the battle of the Coral Sea raged, Admiral Yama-

moto continued his plans for an assault on the island of
Midway, which was to result in one of the most decisive
battles in the Pacific. Yamamoto's goals were twofold: to
capture Midway, further securing Japan's eastern defensive
perimeter; and to draw out and destroy the rest of the U.S.
Pacific Fleet. He assembled a fleet of 165 warships and then
split it into several task forces. Part of the fleet was sent
north to attack the Aleutian Islands in a move primarily
intended to divert American forces from the main Japanese
target. The rest of the ships sailed toward Midway in widely
separated forces.

Yamamoto expected the Pacific Fleet to approach Midway
after his forces had launched their initial attack on the
island; he believed that no American carriers were in the
vicinity. Unknown to Yamamoto, Nimitz's code-breakers
had apprised him of the Japanese plans, and he had rushed
his fleet, including three carriers, to the area before the
Japanese arrived. Nimitz positioned his forces so that they
could be supported by land-based planes on Midway. Admiral Fletcher, who was in tactical command of the defensive operation, led one task force, while Rear Admiral
Raymond A. Spruance headed the other. During the first
phase of the battle, Fletcher turned over command to
Spruance when he was forced to abandon his torpedoed
flagship.

Beginning on June 3, Japanese forces struck in the Aleutians, first bombing U.S. bases at Dutch Harbor and then
seizing the islands of Kiska and Attu (retaken in May 1943).
The main battle of Midway took place June 4–6, with the
Japanese beginning the action by bombing the island. By the
end of the first day, American carrier planes had surprised
the enemy task forces and destroyed all the Japanese carriers.
Yamamoto then tried unsuccessfully to lure the Pacific Fleet
into a surface battle with the powerful battleships and
cruisers he personally commanded to the west, but he
eventually decided to withdraw. Spruance wisely chose not to
pursue Yamamoto's more potent fleet.

The losses for the Japanese at Midway were horrendous: 4 carriers, 275 planes, and 3,500 men killed. In contrast, the Americans lost 1 carrier, 132 planes, and 307 men dead. The destruction of the carriers denied the Japanese the initiative in future operations. In addition, Japan was unable to replace the many experienced pilots who were lost.

By the end of the first six months of the Pacific war, the U.S. navy had rebounded from heavy losses to gain a great triumph at Midway. But during the same time the army suffered one of its severest defeats when the American-Filipino army in the Philippines surrendered to a smaller Japanese force. Japanese planes had first struck bases in the Philippines on December 8, 1941, nine hours after the American command in Manila had received word of the Pearl Harbor attack. In spite of the warning, American forces in the Philippines were no better prepared than those at Pearl Harbor to respond to a Japanese air raid. Half the B-17 bombers and most of the fighters of General Douglas MacArthur's air strength were destroyed on the ground by enemy aircraft, mainly at Clark Field on Luzon.

After earlier landings of small units at isolated locales in the Philippines, the Japanese Fourteenth Army, under the command of Lieutenant General Masaharu Homma, made the main assault on December 22 at Lingayen Gulf in north-western Luzon. A Japanese division landed on the southeast side of the island two days later. The two forces set out to split the defenders by linking up in the Manila area.

Facing them were the U.S. Army Forces, Far East (USAFFE), composed of American and Filipino forces under MacArthur's command. Included were 19,000 American army soldiers, 1,600 marines, 12,000 Philippine Scouts, and 100,000 Philippine army troops. The U.S. Asiatic Fleet left the Philippines for the Netherlands East Indies soon after the initial attack, while nothing remained of the U.S. army air forces on Luzon except for a handful of fighters.

MacArthur followed the dictates of War Plan Orange-3 after an initial attempt to defend all of the archipelago. He ordered a withdrawal of his Luzon forces to the peninsula of Bataan and the island of Corregidor, from which they would attempt to defend Manila Bay. Hoping to spare Manila from destruction, the general declared it an open city, while he moved his headquarters and top Philippine officials to Corregidor on Christmas Eve. The North and South Luzon forces, thanks to a brilliant plan devised by MacArthur and boldly implemented by his troops, managed to evade Homma's efforts to split and trap them. They skillfully withdrew into defensive lines together on the north end of Bataan Peninsula. By January 6, 80,000 American and Filipino troops had completed their retreat to Bataan, where 26,000 Filipino refugees had also arrived. Some defenders also were assigned to Corregidor (and three other small island fortresses) at the entrance to Manila Bay.

The battle for control of the peninsula began on the 9th, with Homma's less experienced troops leading the attack; his best units had been redeployed to Java. Ill-equipped, suffering from inadequate food supplies, and devastated by disease in the rugged, malaria-infested terrain, the Bataan force held out against the Japanese until April 9, 1942. After their surrender, the American-Filipino troops were marched sixty-five miles to prison camps in the infamous "Bataan Death March," during which numerous atrocities were committed against them. Six hundred American and eight thousand Filipino troops died on the march alone, with many more lost later in Japanese prison camps.

The force on Corregidor capitulated on May 6. Major General Jonathan M. Wainwright formally surrendered the Philippines when Homma threatened to kill his defenseless wounded men and nurses in a Corregidor tunnel. The remaining American and Filipino forces in the central and southern Philippines laid down their arms gradually, the last units doing so on June 9. Many American and Filipino soldiers escaped into the countryside and later participated in guerrilla resistance against the Japanese.

Command in the Philippines had passed to Wainwright

on March 11 when MacArthur left the islands upon the orders of President Roosevelt. After a dangerous journey, MacArthur reached southern Australia and, in a famous speech at Adelaide, promised that "I shall return" to liberate the Philippines—though at the time plans for future Allied action against the Japanese were far from certain.

In March 1942 the Combined Chiefs of Staff assigned to the United States the primary strategic responsibility for the Pacific war. At the end of the month the Joint Chiefs of Staff divided the Pacific into two theaters of operation. They appointed MacArthur to head the Southwest Pacific Area (SWPA), which included Australia, the Bismarck Archipelago, part of the Solomon Islands, Papua and Northeast New Guinea, and the Netherlands East Indies, excluding Sumatra. The rest of the Pacific was designated the Pacific Ocean Areas (POA), under the command of Nimitz; it was further subdivided into South, Central, and North Pacific areas. The arrangement represented a compromise between the American army and navy: MacArthur was the more senior commander, but the navy, especially Admiral King, refused to put him in charge of the Pacific Fleet or Central Pacific operations, since to them the war loomed as primarily a naval show.

Following their triumphs in the East Indies and Philippines and their defeat at Midway, the Japanese high command decided to try again to take Port Moresby, the main Allied bastion just north of Australia. The Japanese now planned to land an invasion force on the north coast of Papua, New Guinea, and to reach Port Moresby by crossing the Owen Stanley Mountains. In actions intended to cover the flank of the Papuan action and to cut the line of communications from the United States to Australia, the Japanese also built up bases on Tulagi and Guadalcanal in the southern Solomons.

In July the Joint Chiefs of Staff ordered MacArthur and Nimitz to counter the Japanese actions by launching offensives in Papua and the Solomons, with the ultimate intention of assaulting the Japanese stronghold of Rabaul on New Britain, north of the Solomons. South Pacific Area forces, under Rear Admiral Robert L. Ghormley, were to occupy Guadalcanal and Tulagi in the Solomons, as well as the Santa Cruz islands. The next objectives were to be the capture of the Huon Gulf area of Northeast New Guinea by MacArthur's Australian and American troops and the conquest of the rest of the Solomons by the South Pacific units, which were part of Nimitz's POA theater.

The American invasion of Guadalcanal was set for August 7, under the overall command of Admiral Ghormley. Major General A. Archer Vandegrift's First Marine Division was designated to lead the assaults on Guadalcanal and Tulagi. At the time of the landings, the number of Japanese on the two islands was only 3,700.

Initially the invasions met limited resistance. The capture of Tulagi was completed within several days. The main landing force on Guadalcanal suffered no combat casualties the first day as Japanese troops and workers abandoned the partially built airfield near the north coast, which the marines finished within three weeks and named Henderson Field. Severe supply problems for the American ground forces arose almost immediately, however, when their accompanying ships, fearing attacks by the Japanese navy, suddenly withdrew from Guadalcanal before fully unloading their cargo. The marines were immediately forced to reduce rations.

One important factor in the decision to pull the Allied ships away from Guadalcanal was the night battle of Savo Island, in which four American and Australian cruisers and a destroyer were sunk, and two thousand Allied sailors died in only half an hour. This was the first of seven major naval battles that accompanied the ground struggle for Guadalcanal. For months the Japanese navy controlled the seas around the island by night while the Allies dominated by day. Using a constant stream of vessels from Rabaul nicknamed the "Tokyo Express," the Japanese moved in reinforcements each night to the island. Engaging the marines mainly at night in fierce battles, they were aided by air and naval attacks.

In October the Japanese accelerated their troop convoys and naval bombardments of the American beachhead. Nimitz decided to increase his commitment of troops and of naval and air support, and on October 18 he appointed Vice Admiral William F. Halsey to succeed Ghormley as commander of the South Pacific. Halsey, the aggressive veteran of numerous task force raids in the spring, brought new confidence and energy to the task.

Shortly after he took over, the Japanese launched their last major offensives to drive American forces from Guadalcanal. American firepower was overwhelming in turning back the frontal assaults of the Japanese. The fighting around the marines' defense perimeter, centered on Henderson Field, reached its climax in November with the Japanese losing heavily in piecemeal attacks. Enemy ground strength on Guadalcanal peaked in November at thirty thousand, after which the Japanese slowly retreated to the north end of the island, though not without heavy fighting. The naval battle of Guadalcanal, November 12–15, was the largest sea engagement in the struggle for the island, ending in a costly defeat for the enemy and thereafter the U.S. navy's clear predominance in the waters of the southern Solomons.

In December the malaria-ridden First Marine Division was relieved by army General Alexander Patch's Americal Division. After the addition of one marine and one army division the next month, along with later reinforcements, Patch was named head of the XIV Corps on Guadalcanal. Following powerful offensives by the Americans, whose numbers now stood at 60,000, the Japanese successfully evacuated their remaining 12,000 troops, and the island was secured in early February. The Americans had suffered 5,800 casualties while the Japanese lost 14,800 men in combat and 9,000 to disease.

As the struggle for Guadalcanal raged, the Allies fought

off new Japanese offensives in Papua on the island of New Guinea. On July 21, 1942, Major General Tomitaro Horii's South Seas Force landed at Buna on the north coast in preparation for an overland drive through the Owen Stanley Mountains to Port Moresby on the south coast. Horii's fourteen thousand men followed the rugged Kokoda Trail through the mountains and by July 29 had overwhelmed the small Australian defensive force in the village of Kokoda, located almost halfway to their target.

MacArthur rushed reinforcements to Port Moresby as well as to Milne Bay farther south in Papua, including two veteran Australian divisions and elements of two inexperienced American infantry divisions. As Horii moved slowly through the mountains of Papua, a Japanese amphibious force landed near Milne Bay at the tip of Papua on August 25. The outnumbered invaders were badly defeated by strong Allied defenses in a ten-day battle. On September 17 the Japanese ground forces, now numbering only ten thousand men, advanced to within thirty-two miles of Port Moresby. Crippled by disease and lacking adequate supplies, the Japanese could not overcome the Australian defenders and were forced to withdraw three days later.

MacArthur ordered a counteroffensive to be launched October 1. The Australians, under General Thomas Blamey, set off along the Kokoda Trail in pursuit of Horii's forces; American troops were flown in from the south and were assigned to follow different routes against the fleeing Japanese. During the retreat Horii and a number of his men drowned crossing a mountain river. While the Australians closed in on the Buna area from the west, American regiments advanced toward the enemy stronghold from the south. Lacking support from the U.S. navy, partly because of uncharted waters, MacArthur used Lieutenant General George C. Kenney's Fifth Air Force to transport troops and supplies to the combat zone in Papua.

By the time the Australians and Americans prepared to attack Buna, much of General Hatazo Adachi's Eighteenth

Army was firmly entrenched in the area. The enemy fortifications withstood assault after assault while the Allied soldiers struggled with problems of disease, inadequate supplies, and the inhospitable climate. The progress of the American troops was especially slow, leading MacArthur to send Lieutenant General Robert L. Eichelberger of the U.S. I Corps in Australia to the Papuan front with the instructions, "Go out there, Bob, and take Buna, or don't come back alive." Eichelberger relieved several commanders and assumed overall control of American forces himself in early December.

After six more weeks of savage fighting, the Papuan campaign ended on January 22, 1943. The fight for Guadalcanal had surely been tough and bloody, but the lesser-known battles for Papua had been even costlier. Altogether, 33,000 Australian and American troops had been involved, and 85 percent were hospitalized with disease at some point during the fighting. Allied casualties in the Papuan operations totaled 8,500, including 3,100 killed. American combat casualties were 2,800. One in 33 of the Americans on Guadalcanal lost his life in combat or from disease, but 1 in 11 Allied troops died in the operations in Papua, most in the battle for the Buna area.

Not only had the Japanese drive to take Port Moresby been turned back, but the Allies had successfully taken the offensive and had acquired bases and airfields from which to launch future campaigns. Although the war in the Pacific would not be won easily, by early 1943 the Allies had earned decisive victories on land and sea and had halted the expansion of Japanese power.

11

Accelerating Offensive Operations

IN SPITE OF the Anglo-American priority on defeating Germany first, the pressures of the war with Japan led to the commitment of 374,000 American troops in the Pacific by February 1943, compared with 298,000 in the Mediterranean theater and 107,000 in the United Kingdom. General Mac-Arthur and Admiral Halsey, commanders of the Southwest Pacific and South Pacific theaters, both tried to persuade the Joint Chiefs of Staff in early March to approve large reinforcements for a joint-theater series of operations by their forces, culminating in an assault on the enemy stronghold of Rabaul on New Britain. On March 28, 1943, the JCS authorized Operation Cartwheel, a considerably scaled-down version of the requested plan. It would provide convergence on Rabaul from two axes of advance—MacArthur's troops moving up the New Guinea coast and Halsey's pushing north through the Solomon Islands. The Joint Chiefs, however, warned the two theater chiefs that Cartwheel would have to be carried out largely with the forces they already had.

Before Cartwheel was to begin in June, General Kenney's American and Australian air units won an unusual victory on March 1–3. His land-based bombers, utilizing novel skip-bombing techniques, sank most of a Japanese convoy of troop transports and destroyers that was sailing from Rabaul to Northeast New Guinea. Enemy losses ranged from twelve to twenty ships, besides sixty aircraft destroyed and troop

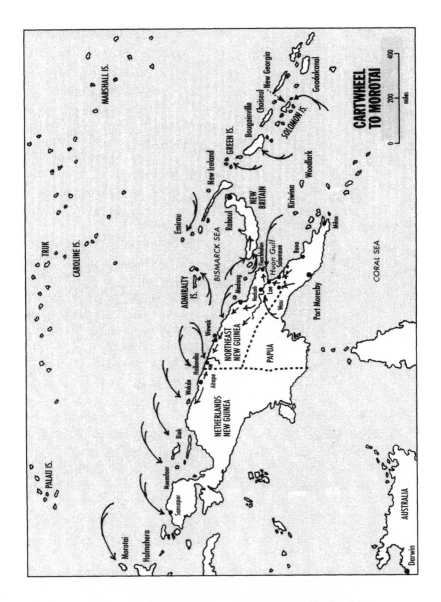

deaths as high as fifteen thousand. Only six Allied planes were lost. Hundreds of Japanese in lifeboats or clinging to debris in the water were strafed to death by Allied PT (patrol torpedo) boats and low-flying planes. Some airmen "confessed to experiencing nausea" as "the terrible yet essential finale" of the battle of the Bismarck Sea took place. "It was a grisly task," commented another, "but a military necessity," for the enemy soldiers "could not be allowed to land and join the Lae garrison" in Northeast New Guinea.

On April 18 Halsey's theater came up with a spectacular feat that matched the Bismarck Sea engagement. That day a group of army P-38 fighters of the South Pacific command, operating on Ultra intercepts, ambushed the plane carrying Admiral Yamamoto over Bougainville in the North Solomons, killing the head of the Japanese Combined Fleet who was also his nation's foremost strategist.

At the Trident Conference in Washington in May, King pointed out how long and costly the Papuan and Guadalcanal campaigns had been and argued for a more direct, economical advance via the Central Pacific, spearheaded by the navy and marines. In radiograms from his headquarters in Brisbane, Australia, MacArthur later crusaded for a single advance to Tokyo from his and Halsey's theaters. He was anxious that Cartwheel go well so that King would not have more ammunition for his case based on slow progress in the Southwest and South Pacific theaters. Regardless of the opening moves in Cartwheel, the Joint Chiefs yielded to King three weeks later and authorized Nimitz to inaugurate a second axis of advance through the Central Pacific, with detailed operational plans to be submitted later. As MacArthur suspected, thereafter the JCS would give logistic and strategic priority in the war against Japan to the Central Pacific.

When Cartwheel went into action on June 30, it set in motion a well-executed series of thirteen major amphibious operations in New Guinea, the Solomons, and the Bismarcks that would wrest control from the Japanese in those regions by the end of March 1944, though bypassing a number of enemy garrisons. Despite their vociferous protests, the two commanders, who had become fast friends, were to be denied their climactic assault on Rabaul. In August the Joint Chiefs, fearing the slaughter of Americans by 100,000 enemy troops at Rabaul, ordered MacArthur and Halsey instead to envelop and isolate the great Japanese stronghold on the eastern end of New Britain.

MacArthur's forces, thanks in part to good information on enemy dispositions and movements, achieved their Cartwheel objectives without directly assaulting many of the strongest Japanese concentrations in their theater. The brunt of the ground operations was borne by the Australian First Army inland in Northeast New Guinea and by Lieutenant General Walter Krueger's U.S. Sixth Army along the coast of Northeast New Guinea, as well as on the Trobriand and Admiralty islands, respectively south and north of New Britain. Some Australian and even Dutch air and sea elements were involved in Cartwheel, but the main support for the ground troops was American, provided by Kenney's Fifth Air Force, Vice Admiral Arthur S. Carpender's Seventh Fleet, and Rear Admiral Daniel E. Barbey's VII Amphibious Force.

For the Australians, lengthy, bloody battles ensued at Wau and Salamaua, but the Americans were fortunate in capturing their main objectives, Lae and Finschhafen on the Huon Gulf, without large-scale fighting. The Lae operation involved the first major airborne drop in the Pacific conflict. Observed by MacArthur in his B-17 on September 5, an American parachute infantry regiment dropped at Nadzab, a short distance northwest of Lae. The paratroopers quickly secured the area, moving on to join up with Australian and American divisions that had advanced from the west and south. Together they captured the principal Japanese base in the Huon region, Lae, on September 16.

Adachi's Japanese Eighteenth Army, regrouped and revitalized since the Buna fight, was the main enemy force on the Huon Peninsula but was unable to stop either the subsequent Australian drive northwest from Lae up the Markham Valley or the American capture of Finschhafen by two-pronged overland and amphibious assaults in early October 1943. The conquest of the peninsula was completed in January when an American task force took Saidor on the northern coast in a seaborne assault and pushed inland to make contact with advancing Australians. Adachi shifted his remaining units up the coast to make stands at Madang and Wewak along the coast of Northeast New Guinea.

Meanwhile, in December 1943, Southwest Pacific troops had landed on the west end of New Britain. The U.S. First Cavalry Division seized Arawe on the southwest coast, and the First Marine Division assaulted Cape Gloucester on the northwest end of the island two weeks later. Eventually the Americans pushed eastward halfway to Rabaul, and later Australian troops replaced them. In a smart strategic move, MacArthur sent the First Cavalry Division to the Admiralty Islands, located north of Rabaul across the Bismarck Sea. The cavalrymen assaulted Los Negros on February 29 and nearby Manus on March 15, securing those two main islands of the Admiralties after short but severe battles. Not only was Rabaul now isolated, but the American air bases and harbor in the Admiralties would be important to future invasions.

Halsey's portion of Cartwheel was implemented simultaneously with MacArthur's. His principal ground, sea, and air forces were American, with some New Zealand support: Lieutenant General Oscar W. Griswold's U.S. Army XIV Corps, Halsey's Third Fleet, Major General Roy S. Geiger's I Marine Amphibious Corps, Rear Admiral Theodore S. "Pug" Wilkinson's III Amphibious Force, and Major General Nathan F. Twining's Thirteenth Air Force. Opposing the Cartwheel offensives in the Central and North Solomons was Lieutenant General Haruyoshi Hyakutake's Seventeenth Army, together with surface, submarine, and air elements from Truk and Rabaul.

From late June through October 1943, South Pacific forces were occupied in the conquest of the Central Solomons. One of the severest actions was the battle for Munda Point on New Georgia, where the enemy had an air base surrounded by formidable defenses. Difficult terrain, tropical weather and diseases, and continuing reinforcements that poured down "the Slot" through the Solomons from Rabaul all added to the Americans' difficulties on New Georgia. Also, American naval ships providing offshore gunfire support for the troops faced uncharted waters and two sharp but inconclusive engagements against the Japanese navy: the battles of Kula Gulf and Kolombangara, both in July. Munda Point was secured on August 5, but the mopping up on New Georgia took until early October. American casualties were 1,100 killed and 3,900 wounded, while the Japanese lost 2,500 killed, with both sides suffering heavy casualties from the many tropical diseases common to the area. It was off one of the islands near New Georgia that PT-109 was sunk on August 1, though Lieutenant John F. Kennedy and most of his crew survived. When American troops launched amphibious assaults on two nearby islands, the Japanese navy tried to evacuate those garrisons, which set off two more naval battles—an American victory in August and a triumph for the Japanese in October, their last naval victory of the war.

In late October Halsey sent an American and New Zealand force to take the lightly held Treasury Islands and a U.S. marine battalion to raid Choiseul, both operations occurring south of Bougainville, the impending final major invasion in the Solomons. Rear Admiral R. Kelly Turner, a close friend of Nimitz, now commanded the III Amphibious Force, which transported the Third Marine Division to Bougainville for the assault on November 1. General Vandegrift led the I Marine Amphibious Corps ashore at Empress Augusta Bay and began to establish a strong defensive perimeter. "Seabees" (construction battalions) rapidly built an air base at the beachhead while an army division joined the marine division that arrived first. On November 9 Geiger succeeded Vandegrift, who returned to Washington to become commandant of the Marine Corps. About forty thousand enemy troops of the Seventeenth Army were on the east, north, and south coasts. Their scattered locations on the 130-mile-long island prevented orderly concentration for

effective attacks against the perimeter on the west coast at
Empress Augusta Bay.

As in earlier amphibious assaults, the U.S. navy soon
found itself engaged by enemy naval units: the battles of
Empress Augusta Bay on November 2 and of Cape Saint
George on the 25th. Both were won handily by the Americans. Halsey and MacArthur then teamed to strike Rabaul
with carrier and land-based aircraft, respectively, wreaking
havoc on planes and ships at the Japanese stronghold, the
source of most reinforcements for the Solomons defenders.

Fierce fighting on Bougainville continued until the end of
1943, by which time the American perimeter extended five
miles inland and six miles along the coast. It contained more
than 44,000 American troops, including another army division that replaced the marines. The beachhead was filled
with heavy guns and good fortifications, and the Torokina
air base was in heavy use; soon two bomber fields were
added. When in mid-March 1944 the Japanese launched
their last major attack against the Americans, Griswold's
ground troops numbered 60,000 and the Japanese 16,000.
The nine-day battle cost the XIV Corps 1,800 casualties, but
the Japanese lost more than 8,000.

No further attempt was made by the Americans to
enlarge the perimeter; it served its purpose quite well as it
was, and there was no danger of the enemy overrunning it.
Halsey had made a wise decision to resist conquering the
whole of Bougainville. Inexplicably, MacArthur later approved an expensive operation by the Australians to eliminate the bypassed Japanese there.

Halsey's forces finished their part of Cartwheel rather
anticlimactically with two minor operations, taking the
Green Islands above Bougainville in mid-February and Emi-
rau, northeast of New Britain, on March 20. Later that
spring Halsey joined Central Pacific operations as commander of the Third Fleet, and the South Pacific theater
was deactivated as a combat zone. His army and army
air force elements went to the Southwest Pacific theater,

and his navy and marine elements were transferred to the Central Pacific. Cartwheel had been well planned and smartly executed by MacArthur's and Halsey's staffs and field forces. Allied personnel visiting Rabaul after the war were impressed by its extensive fortifications, many tunnels, and huge numbers of trapped Japanese personnel. The Joint Chiefs' decision to bypass Rabaul was surely one of their wisest moves.

By the early autumn of 1943, Nimitz commanded an enormous and still growing array of ground, sea, and air power for his long-awaited Central Pacific offensive. His Fifth Fleet, led by Vice Admiral Raymond A. Spruance, perhaps Nimitz's most trusted commander, was already the largest fleet in American history but doubled in size before the war ended. The V Amphibious Force, headed by Admiral Turner, transported the ground forces, organized under the V Amphibious Corps and commanded by marine Major General Holland M. "Howlin' Mad" Smith. The V Corps included two army and two marine divisions, though only elements of two divisions would see combat in the first Central Pacific operation, the invasion of the Gilbert Islands.

Nimitz believed the conquest of some of the Gilberts was essential to build air bases so that the next move, into the Marshalls, could have land-based air support. Marine General Smith, known for his volatile nature and blunt opinions, countered futilely that the Gilberts should be bypassed and the Marshalls invaded first. The two islands of the Gilberts chosen for assault were Tarawa and Makin; both were atolls, or clusters of small islands with coral reefs offshore.

After an eight-day bombardment by naval guns and army bombers that did not damage enemy defenses as much as anticipated, the assaults began on November 20. Major General Ralph Smith's Twenty-seventh Infantry Division took four days to secure Makin, though there were only 500 Japanese troops and 200 Korean laborers. Only 100, mostly Koreans, survived. American casualties were 70 killed and 150 wounded. Marine General Smith was critical of the army's slow progress, which subjected the naval ships to submarine attacks. An escort carrier was sunk off Makin, with 640 of its sailors killed. It was not a happy beginning for the two Smiths, who would collide again the next summer on Saipan.

To the south in the Tarawa atoll, Major General Julian C. Smith's Second Marine Division invaded the tiny island of Betio. It seemed, however, that the 4,700 Japanese troops had fortified every square yard. The coral reef off Betio proved too shallow for the assault craft, so most of the marines had to wade hundreds of yards to the beach amid intense enemy fire. On the first day 1,500 marines died or were wounded. Daily progress was often measured in a few yards, so fanatical was the Japanese resistance. Except for 100 prisoners, of whom only 17 were combat troops, all the Betio defenders were killed in action. Marine losses shocked the high commands in Pearl Harbor and Washington, as well as the American public when it was belatedly informed: nearly 1,000 dead and 2,200 wounded to secure three-hundred-acre Betio. Tarawa ranks among the bloodiest American battles in the proportion of casualties to troops involved, but it provided air bases in supporting the Marshalls invasion. It also gave Nimitz's assault leaders and forces many valuable lessons in amphibious warfare.

For the Marshalls invasion, Nimitz and his planners agreed to hit the Kwajalein atoll, with the Seventh Infantry and Fourth Marine divisions attacking islands fifty miles apart yet within the atoll's bounds. On February 1, 1944, the army division assaulted Kwajalein Island, at the southeast end of the atoll, while the marines landed on Roi and Namur islands on the north central edge of the atoll. All the islands were secured by February 7. Spruance, Turner, and Holland Smith, the key American commanders over the operations, were pleased with the improvement in fire support, logistics, intelligence data, and the troops' conduct in combat. American losses were 370 killed and 1,000 wounded out of 41,000 troops engaged. Nearly all the 8,000 Japanese

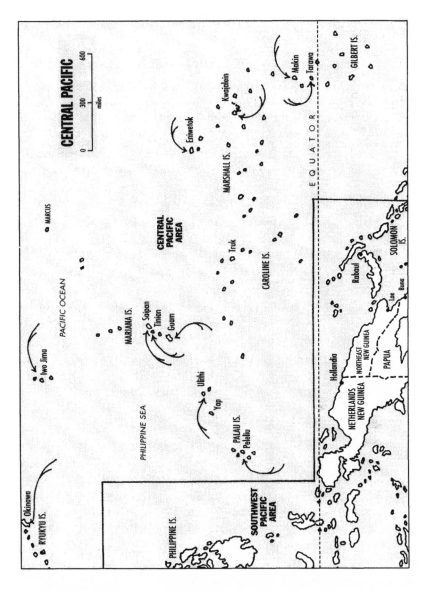

were killed, only 130 being taken prisoner. The three-day pre-assault bombardments by aircraft and surface ships had been much more accurate and devastating than those at Tarawa.

Eniwetok and nearby Parry Island were the final Marshalls operations. The two islands lie on the far northwest corner of the archipelago. It took a marine regiment and several army battalions four days to annihilate the 2,200 defenders.

By that time Rear Admiral Marc A. Mitscher's Fast Carrier Force, which was Task Force 58 of the Fifth Fleet, had 12 carriers, accompanied by a powerful array of battleships, cruisers, and destroyers, to decimate any support efforts from Japanese-held islands for many miles in all directions. His 900 or more aircraft were backed by well-coordinated land-based air missions from the Gilberts. On February 17, as Eniwetok was assaulted, Mitscher's carrier planes raided Truk, destroying 200,000 tons of shipping and 275 aircraft, with few American losses. Truk would be hit many times again, but as the JCS had decided, it would not be invaded. Interestingly, the Japanese high command sent no more reinforcements to Truk; they too were obviously aware of its vulnerability.

In the Southwest Pacific in the spring of 1944, MacArthur decided to use his American Sixth Army in a surprise 550-mile leap from the Huon Peninsula along the north coast to Hollandia in Netherlands New Guinea. While the Australian First Army moved toward Madang, where Adachi's Eighteenth Army headquarters and largest forces were located, two divisions of the U.S. Sixth Army landed on either side of Hollandia against light opposition on April 22. Excellent firepower and logistical support was provided by Barbey's VII Amphibious Force, Vice Admiral Thomas C. Kinkaid's Seventh Fleet, Mitscher's Fast Carrier Force (on loan from the Fifth Fleet), and Kenney's Fifth Air Force. Quickly seizing the Hollandia area, Krueger's forces killed 5,000 enemy troops while losing only 100 Americans killed and 1,000 wounded. The same day one of Krueger's divisions landed 150 miles east of Hollandia at Aitape. There 450 Americans were killed and 2,500 wounded, while 9,000 enemy troops died in the two-day battle for the Aitape area. With the securing of the Hollandia-Aitape region,

MacArthur had trapped the Japanese Eighteenth Army, caught now between the Americans on the west and the Australians approaching from the south and east. On May 17 Krueger's troops captured Wakde Island, west of Hollandia, but it proved unsuitable for bomber bases. MacArthur then chose Biak Island, which lay on the north end of Geelvink Bay and had several good airfields. An amphibious assault by a Sixth Army division on May 27 began a battle against a well-entrenched Japanese garrison of 10,000 that lasted until June 29. As at Buna, Eichelberger had to be brought in to succeed the divisional commander and strong reinforcements had to be summoned before the fighting on Biak turned in favor of the Sixth Army soldiers. All the defenders died in the savage action, which cost the Americans more than 2,700 killed and wounded.

Perhaps the least-known major engagement of the Pacific war was the battle of the Driniumor River, which lasted from July 10 to August 25 in the jungles and marshes around the river that entered the ocean twenty miles east of Aitape. Forced westward by the advancing Australian First Army, Adachi's Japanese Eighteenth Army moved toward the American defenses, which had been carefully prepared along the west bank of the Driniumor. Major General Charles P. Hall's XI Corps took the brunt of Adachi's fierce and continuing assaults, which continued with only brief intervals for nearly six weeks.

Krueger and Hall had the enormous advantage of Ultra intercepts that yielded valuable information on the Japanese units' plans and movements. When the battered remnants of Adachi's army began retreating from the Driniumor in early August, Hall undertook a double envelopment—simultaneous drives around both enemy flanks—which trapped many of the Japanese. The rest fell back fifteen miles east of the Driniumor, but Hall decided not to pursue. Instead his soldiers completed the mop-up of the Driniumor battleground and strengthened defensive lines in the area. The Driniumor battle cost the Japanese ten thousand soldiers killed; Hall's reinforced corps suffered three thousand casualties. Henceforth Adachi's army was never a threat to the Hollandia-Aitape area. There MacArthur developed a large complex of ground and air facilities that became important for air support and the staging of later operations as far north as the Philippines.

The final operations in the conquest of Dutch New Guinea were two minor amphibious assaults in July: Noemfoor Island, west of Biak; and Sansapor, on the northwest tip of New Guinea's Vogelkop Peninsula. That autumn Australian troops conducted further mopping-up operations against scattered small elements of Japanese in Northeast New Guinea, New Britain, and Bougainville. MacArthur's last operation below the Philippines was an amphibious attack in mid-September by Hall's troops on lightly held Morotai in the Halmahera Islands, northwest of New Guinea. More than three hundred enemy defenders were killed, with the remaining few taken prisoner. Only thirty-one American soldiers were killed. The Morotai operation is considered "one of the most economic and worthwhile undertakings of the Southwest Pacific war" because the air bases built on the island were heavily used in the advance into the Philippines.

MacArthur's forces' achievements from April to September 1944 had been considerable: 1,600 combat deaths among his forces, which killed more than 26,400 Japanese and advanced more than 1,400 miles from Northeast New Guinea to the Halmaheras. In the same period Nimitz's forces, operating usually against larger enemy units and stronger fortifications, had advanced 2,600 miles but sometimes with frightful casualties.

12

From Saipan to Burma

FROM THE TIME he proposed the near disastrous
invasion of Guadalcanal, Admiral King had become increasingly convinced that the most indispensable operation in the
Pacific was the conquest of the Marianas. The islands, which
lay only thirteen hundred miles from Japan, had to be taken,
he reasoned, because of their potentially immense value. A
large-scale B-29 strategic bombing program against Japan
could be launched from there; the enemy line of communications to Southeast Asia could be cut by air and sea forces
operating from the Marianas; and invasions of Formosa and
then Japan could be largely staged from those islands.
Nimitz also came to regard the Marianas operations as
strategically the most significant of the Pacific War.

Operation Forager, the Marianas invasion, provided for
three key islands—Saipan, Tinian, and Guam—to be seized
and the other twelve of the archipelago to be isolated. In
early planning the three were judged the best for air and
naval base development. Nimitz appointed his most depend-
able, experienced top commanders to the highest posts for
Forager: Spruance over the Fifth Fleet, Turner over the
Marianas Joint Expeditionary Force, and Holland Smith
over the entire Marianas ground operations and the Saipan
assault directly. Smith's V Amphibious Corps consisted of
two marine divisions and one army, which would stage from
Hawaii, 3,500 miles to the east. Forager ground forces would

have the strong fire support of Mitscher's now huge Fast Carrier Force and the powerful Fifth Fleet's guns.

Japanese personnel on Saipan numbered thirty thousand. Lieutenant General Yoshisugu Saito commanded the army troops, about two-thirds of the total, while Vice Admiral Chuichi Nagumo, who had led the Pearl Harbor Attack Force, headed the naval personnel on the island. The Japanese had been building an elaborate defense system but had only partly completed their fortifications by the time the Americans landed. Four days earlier, when naval and air bombardments began, the battleships included four bombed at Pearl Harbor and later salvaged or repaired—an ironic twist since the head of the Pearl Harbor attackers was on Saipan.

The Second and Fourth Marine divisions assaulted the southwest shore of Saipan on June 15. Opposition was fierce, and on the first day the marines moved only halfway to their day's objective, losing two thousand casualties. On the second day the army's Twenty-seventh Infantry Division landed on the southern beachhead where fighting was still heavy. Saito and Nagumo had launched early strong counterattacks, hoping to drive the Americans back into the sea. The uncoordinated, piecemeal nature of the Japanese attacks and extraordinary American firepower allowed U.S. forces to establish a firm beachhead and to start expanding it aggressively.

The day the Saipan invasion began, Spruance learned that Vice Admiral Jisaburo Ozawa's First Mobile Fleet had turned from its planned attack on MacArthur's forces in Dutch New Guinea and was speeding toward the Marianas. The Guam assault, set for June 18, was postponed, while Nimitz ordered Mitscher's powerful Task Force 58, built around the Pacific Fleet's enormous and still-growing number of carriers, to block the Japanese fleet from entering the Marianas vicinity and to destroy as many enemy ships and aircraft as possible.

On June 19, the first day of the battle of the Philippine Sea, Ozawa hurled three large air attacks against Mitscher's force. In an eight-hour period, 350 Japanese aircraft were shot down and only 30 U.S. planes were lost in the "Great Marianas Turkey Shoot." Later that same day American submarines and planes sank three enemy carriers, including Ozawa's flagship (he escaped) and two other vessels. The attacks also damaged another carrier and destroyed 65 enemy aircraft. Only 20 American planes were shot down, but 80 others were lost in ditchings or crash landings as they tried to return to their carriers that night.

With no American ships lost by the 21st, Spruance issued a controversial order for Mitscher's force not to pursue the retreating Japanese vessels. Instead he wanted them to return to covering and supporting the troops on Saipan. Ozawa's badly crippled fleet was allowed to escape, but Spruance maintained his priority on the Saipan operation, a decision firmly backed by Nimitz and King. The battle of the Philippine Sea cost the Japanese navy its last large body of trained naval airmen, and it cut off the Saipan defenders from any outside assistance.

Meanwhile, on Saipan the marine divisions advanced slowly into the mountainous central region while the army division captured the southern area of the island and then moved into the middle of the line as the three divisions pushed north. Encountering heavy enemy fire in "Death Valley," as it became known, General Ralph Smith's army soldiers could not keep pace, thus exposing the inner flanks of the marine divisions on either side of Smith's troops. On June 24 marine General "Howlin' Mad" Smith set off a furor from Saipan to Washington by relieving army General Ralph Smith. At issue were sharp differences between army and marine tactics as well as the startling act of a marine general's firing of an army general.

After intense combat and heavy casualties on both sides, the American divisions moved into northern Saipan in early July. Banzai attacks (suicidal charges) became frequent, the largest hitting the army sector on the night of July 6–7; by sunrise the Japanese had lost 4,300 troops. After more savage battles on the north end of the island, Turner declared on

July 9 that Saipan was secured. During the last hours of hostilities General Saito and Admiral Nagumo committed suicide.

American losses on Saipan almost doubled the total for the operations on Tinian and Guam. Saipan's casualties rank it with Tarawa and Peleliu as the highest proportionate losses for American troops in the Pacific: 3,300 killed or missing and 11,000 wounded. Japanese casualties included 29,000 combat deaths and a handful of prisoners. In addition, hundreds or perhaps thousands of Japanese soldiers and Saipan civilians leapt to their deaths from the high cliffs of Marpi Point at the north end of the island onto large, jagged rocks below. Called by the official marine chronicle "The Crowning Horror," the mass suicides were sadly unpreventable. During the next few days American boats had difficulty moving near Marpi Point "because of the hundreds of corpses floating in the water."

Marine General Smith later called the Saipan operation "the decisive battle of the Pacific offensive." Nine days after the island was taken, Japanese Prime Minister Hideki Tojo and his whole cabinet resigned because of the "unprecedently great national crisis" produced by the loss of Saipan. The Americans quickly began huge construction projects on the island. Most important were two large B-29 bases, which began receiving the big bombers in October. The first B-29 mission against Tokyo was November 24. Saipan was also significant to the seizure of nearby Tinian.

Guam, over twice the size of Saipan, is the largest and southernmost of the Marianas. It had been ceded by Spain to the United States in 1898. Its invasion marked the first liberation of United States territory during the war. The Japanese had conquered the island on December 10, 1941, after a stiff but brief battle pitting 6,000 invaders against the 420-man American garrison, aided by Guam natives. The residents were subjected to a moderate military occupation until 1944, when the native men were forced into labor battalions and treated like slaves during the frantic construction of fortifications in anticipation of an American invasion. The Southern Task Force (Guam) of Operation Forager was led by Rear Admiral Richard L. Connolly, with marine General Roy Geiger in charge of the III Amphibious Corps, consisting of a division and a brigade of marines as well as an army division. The pre-assault bombardments lasted thirteen days—the heaviest yet in the Pacific conflict. The marines landed on two widely separated beaches on the west side of Guam on July 21, 1944. Strong enemy opposition cost more than 1,000 casualties the first day, and part of the army division had to be sent into combat. The Americans, still facing savage resistance, began to move inland and along the coast, linking the two beachheads less than a week later. One of the wildest actions occurred when enemy banzai attacks hit the marines on Orote Peninsula, where the main Japanese air base was located. On the night of July 25–26 marines killed 3,500 banzai chargers but suffered 800 casualties of their own.

Major General Takeshi Takashima, in charge of the defense of Guam, had nineteen thousand soldiers, including a veteran division of the war in China, and a good supply of heavy guns and munitions. He had presciently placed most of his troops along the west coast, which was where the Americans landed. He was killed in action soon after ordering his soldiers to withdraw into the interior mountains and jungles. Major General Hideyoshi Obata, who succeeded him, led the Japanese forces to the northeast corner of Guam for a last-ditch stand. In the ensuing heavy fighting, mostly in rough country, the Japanese were slowly destroyed or scattered into small groups; Obata was killed in action. Geiger announced on August 10 the end of organized resistance on the island. A few Japanese, still believing the war was under way, hid in the wild interior until 1962 when the supposedly final two soldiers were discovered and returned home to Japan.

American losses on Guam were 2,100 dead and 5,700 wounded or missing in action. Nearly 90 percent of these were marines, who faced the heaviest sustained action. Nearly all the Japanese troops were killed; a few were taken prisoner. Guam's Apra Harbor became the focal point of a large complex of American naval and air installations, including in early 1945 Nimitz's Pacific Ocean Areas (POA) headquarters. Guam was to be used for basing B-29s and for supporting the Iwo Jima and Okinawa operations.

The final phase of Forager was the invasion of Tinian, which began July 21 after thirty-three days of pre-assault bombardment, the longest of the war against Japan. General Holland Smith, who had taken command of the Fleet Marine Force, Pacific, at Pearl Harbor, accompanied the Tinian armada since he had been a key planner of the operation. Marine General Harry Schmidt succeeded him over the Tinian invaders, consisting of two marine divisions and an army division in reserve. Rear Admiral Harry Hill's Northern Attack Force transported the marines to the northwestern coast of Tinian, which could be covered by American field artillery on Saipan as well as by Hill's naval guns. Colonel Takashi Ogata's eight thousand Japanese on Tinian were well equipped and trained but were surprised by the location of the American assault; they had expected it to be at Tinian Town to the southwest.

While Hill's ships pretended to be preparing for an amphibious assault on Tinian Town and led Ogata to rush reinforcements into that area, the marines landed on a tiny beach on the rocky northwest shore and quickly secured the nearby higher ground. In the dark early morning hours of the 25th, Japanese soldiers attacked with banzai charges. In about three hours the marines killed more than twelve hundred of the wild-charging troops. Later that day the other marine division came ashore, and the two divisions swiftly and methodically overran the island, encountering some resistance but never as fanatical as on the first night. Napalm bombs were used by American planes for the first time in the Pacific struggle. The marines took Tinian Town on July 30 and secured the island two days later.

Tinian became the busiest of the B-29 base complexes. B-29s flew from there when they dropped the atomic bombs on Hiroshima and Nagasaki. Holland Smith, no easy critic, pronounced Tinian "the perfect amphibious operation." An official historian concludes, "As an exercise in amphibious skill it must be given a superior rating, and as a demonstration of ingenuity, it stands as second to no other landing in the Pacific war."

While Spruance's Fifth Fleet was occupied in the Marianas, Nimitz brought Halsey back from the South Pacific to plan for the coming naval role in the Palau Islands. Halsey was to head the Third Fleet, as the Pacific Fleet was now redesignated. His fleet was also to support MacArthur's invasion of Mindanao, the southernmost Philippine island. In mid-September the Fifth Fleet senior command of Spruance, Turner, Smith, and Mitscher returned to Pearl Harbor to plan future Central Pacific operations. Their places were taken, respectively, by Halsey as Third Fleet commander, Wilkinson as head of III Amphibious Force, Geiger as leader of III Amphibious Corps, and Rear Admiral John R. "Slew" McCain as commander of the Fast Carrier Forces (now Task Force 38).

Meanwhile, Roosevelt, Churchill, and the Combined Chiefs of Staff were debating strategy at the Second Quebec Conference. After Nimitz and MacArthur approved, Halsey persuaded Nimitz to notify the American Joint Chiefs at Quebec that Third Fleet planes had just raided the Philippines and found the central islands to be "a hollow shell with weak defenses and skimpy facilities." Halsey, through Nimitz, urged the JCS to drop plans for seizing Yap and the Palau Islands, east of the Philippines. He proposed that the ground forces intended for those assaults be used by MacArthur to invade Leyte in the Central Philippines as soon as possible, instead of Mindanao to the south in November. Nimitz concurred in all of Halsey's recommendations except one, and the JCS quickly approved the POA theater chief's requests. The exception was the Palaus invasion, which

Nimitz insisted on executing, though he probably later regretted it as did the American troops sent there.

The First Marine Division, supported by the Third Fleet and its carrier aircraft, landed on Peleliu in the Palau Islands on September 15, the same day MacArthur's troops assaulted Morotai. Despite a three-day pre-assault bombardment by Halsey's planes and ships, the marines ran into stiff enemy resistance and strong fortifications. The marines also encountered a new enemy tactic of withdrawing from the beaches that were exposed to naval gunfire and of defending from interior ridges and a maze of more than five hundred interconnected caves with well-camouflaged entrances. The defenders numbered ten thousand, mostly from a well-disciplined, experienced division. For the marines, Peleliu involved some of the fiercest fighting of the war. In a critical stage of the battle Geiger had to send in an army regiment as well. The island was not secured until November 25, with mopping up continuing until February 1945.

Peleliu cost ten thousand American casualties, of whom two thousand were killed in action. The enemy garrison was virtually wiped out. Bloody Peleliu was almost worthless in staging or supporting future invasions of the Central Pacific Forces. Its Japanese garrison probably could not have threatened MacArthur's flank during his Leyte invasion. The terrible fight for Peleliu makes the ground hallowed for the many Americans who fell in combat, but the operation itself may have been the most unnecessary of the Pacific war.

The other assaults in the Palaus were made by the Eighty-first Infantry Division. It invaded Angaur Island, near Peleliu, on September 17 and secured it three days later against light resistance. On September 23 army elements seized distant Ulithi Island to the north, which had no Japanese garrison. Ironically, Ulithi, which produced no casualties, provided the Pacific Fleet with one of its finest anchorages for staging future operations.

It is a distant leap to move from the American-dominated war of maritime strategy in the Pacific to the war of

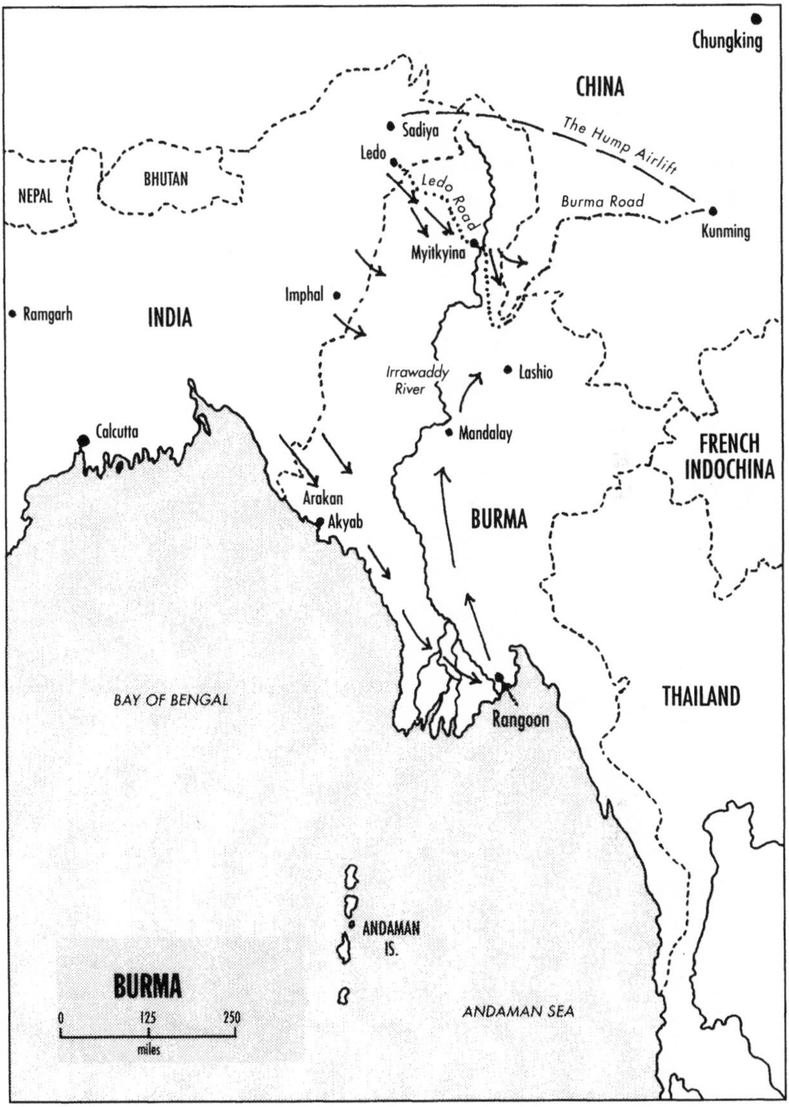
Chungking
CHINA
The Hump Airlift
Sadiya
Ledo
Ledo Road
Burma Road
Kunming
NEPAL
BHUTAN
Myitkyina
Imphal
Ramgarh
INDIA
Irrawaddy River
Lashio
Calcutta
Mandalay
FRENCH INDOCHINA
Arakan
Akyab
BURMA
BAY OF BENGAL
Rangoon
THAILAND
ANDAMAN IS.
BURMA
0
125
250
miles
ANDAMAN SEA

continental strategy in China, Burma, and India (CBI), where Chinese and British commanders and forces had the paramount roles. A half-year before the Pearl Harbor attack, Colonel Claire L. Chennault, with Roosevelt's and Arnold's approval, had established the American Volunteer Group, or

"Flying Tigers," to allow former American navy, marine, and army pilots to help in the defense of China and Burma. They used primarily American-made P-40 fighters and achieved an outstanding record against Japanese bombers. In mid-1942 Chennault's organization, now under Arnold, became the China Air Task Force and was expanded.

Out of this evolved the U.S. Fourteenth Air Force in March 1943, which Chennault led until the final months of the war. By then heavy and medium bombers, along with other types of aircraft needed in the CBI air war, were added in considerable numbers. They flew missions as far as Hankow and Hong Kong in East China, Hainan and Formosa off the China coast, and even the South China Sea. Along with long-range American submarines and MacArthur's bombers, the Fourteenth was important in producing a steady attrition of enemy shipping from Japan to Southeast Asia by way of the South China Sea. Chennault's transports, as well as those of the U.S. Tenth Air Force in India, flew much-needed munitions, supplies, and fuel into China over "The Hump," a dangerous route over the Himalaya Mountains.

The final American air organization sent to the CBI was indeed unique. The Twentieth Air Force consisted of the new B-29 "Superfortresses," which had the longest range of any bombers yet. Its XX Bomber Command, headed by Major General Curtis E. LeMay, was based in South Central China and conducted raids from Singapore to Kyushu, Japan. LeMay was transferred to the Marianas in January 1945, and three months later the XX Bomber Command joined the XXI Bomber Command in the strategic bombing offensive against Japan from those islands. The movement of the last B-29s from China was occasioned by the start of a huge Japanese offensive on the mainland that threatened to overrun their bases.

In early 1942 Lieutenant General Joseph W. Stilwell was sent by Marshall to Burma as commander of the newly created China-Burma-India Theater of Operations, U.S.

Army. Stilwell, who had justifiably earned the nickname "Vinegar Joe," was a crack soldier and China expert, but his assigned tasks were too many for any commander to fulfill. Simultaneously he served as the CBI theater chief of American ground and air forces; Lend-Lease administrator for China; chief of staff to Generalissimo Chiang Kai-shek of the Nationalist regime in China; deputy commander of British Vice Admiral Louis Mountbatten's Southeast Asia command, which based out of India and Ceylon from fall 1943 onward; commander of the Northern Burma Combat Command Area of mainly Chinese and a few American troops; and deputy commander of the Burma Front, which was brilliantly headed by British General William Slim. The top British and Chinese civilian and military leaders in the CBI region did not get along well, nor did Stilwell enjoy harmonious relations with Chiang, Mountbatten, or especially Chennault, his American air chief.

Stilwell arrived in Burma in time to participate in a long march out of Burma in the spring of 1942 as strong Japanese ground forces pushed to the border of India. After prying several Nationalist divisions from Chiang, who was reluctant to lose troops from his fronts in China against the Japanese and the Communist Chinese, Stilwell opened several training bases in eastern India, the largest at Ramgarh. He proved to be an excellent trainer-reformer for the Chinese there, turning them from unreliable, ineffective fighters into combat-ready soldiers of good caliber. As Chiang's chief of staff, he also tried, vainly, to improve the combat readiness of the whole Nationalist Chinese Army.

In late 1943 Stilwell and Slim launched limited offensives into West Burma. The former's force included two Chinese divisions and some Americans, notably Brigadier General Frank D. Merrill's reinforced army regiment, soon to be famous as "Merrill's Marauders." To the south, Slim's troops consisted largely of Indian and British troops, including colorful Brigadier Orde Wingate's division-size Special Forces of Indians, which were nicknamed the "Chindits" and rivaled Merrill's outfit as the most daring raiders in the war in Burma. Lieutenant General Shozo Kawabe headed the Burma Area Army, which comprised two armies—one pitted against Stilwell in the north and the other facing Slim in the south.

Initial offensives in the winter of 1943–1944 were disappointing, with Slim's men achieving significant progress only along the Arakan coast beside the Bay of Bengal. Fighting was heavy on both fronts, resulting in a temporary stalemate. From January through April 1944 Stilwell's Chinese and American troops fought their way through the jungles and mountains of the Hukawng region of Northwest Burma, securing positions for an advance on Stilwell's main objective, the Japanese stronghold of Myitkyina in North Central Burma.

In late April, despite heavy casualties, terrible terrain, and difficult weather, Stilwell launched his long-planned offensive to take the strategically located Myitkyina area. By mid-May the main enemy airfield on the edge of the town had been captured, but enemy reinforcements soon arrived. The main battle for Myitkyina, really a siege, lasted from May 18 to August 3 when the Allies finally drove the starving remnants of the defense force into the jungles. The action cost Stilwell's troops more than five thousand casualties; three thousand Japanese were killed and large numbers died from disease and starvation. Stilwell had finally accomplished his main mission in Burma, which surprised many Allied leaders who thought Myitkyina was an impossible goal for his soldiers.

Stilwell set off on his final drive on October 15, aiming at the key enemy rail corridor in North Burma. His forces, now including a crack British division, five Chinese divisions, and an American brigade, besides two artillery units, at first made good progress. Suddenly, on October 18, he was relieved of his command, an incident fraught with controversy ever since.

For a long time Chiang, his top subordinates, and even

Chennault had wanted Stilwell removed, so poor were their relations with the obstinate but able "Vinegar Joe," who referred to Chiang in private as "the Peanut" and often showed open contempt for his opponents. The opportunity to get rid of Stilwell came when the Japanese began an 820,000-man offensive from May to December 1944 that swept through a large portion of Southeast China, overrunning Chinese cities and armies as well as some B-29 bases. Chiang complained to Roosevelt that if the Chinese divisions Stilwell used in his Myitkyina campaign had been available, Japanese General Yasugi Okamura's well-executed offensive would have been contained—a doubtful premise in view of the poor training and equipment of the Nationalist divisions. Fearing that China might collapse and sue for separate peace terms with Japan, FDR, in spite of Marshall's steadfast defense of the CBI commander, decided to recall Stilwell just as his new drive in Burma was beginning. Major General Albert C. Wedemeyer succeeded him as head of the new China Theater, and Lieutenant General Daniel I. Sultan became head of the India-Burma theater in the reorganization of Stilwell's old CBI theater.

Under Wedemeyer and Sultan until the end of hostilities, the Americans played a decreasing role in strategy and operations. American army engineers planned and supervised the building of the Ledo Road (later renamed the Stilwell Road) across North Burma from India to Kunming in Southwest China, completing that replacement for the prewar Burma Road in January 1945. Although the B-29 groups had been sent to the Marianas to be used solely against Japan's home islands, the Tenth and Fourteenth Air Forces continued conventional bombing missions in the CBI region, together with tactical support of the ground forces in Burma and China. Slim's final campaign in the spring of 1945 completed the liberation of Burma.

Meanwhile, Marshall used Stilwell's great experience and knowledge to good advantage. In the fall of 1944 Stilwell was named commander of all U.S. Army Ground Forces, succeeding Lieutenant General Lesley J. McNair, who had been killed by American bombers during the breakout in Normandy in July 1944. Stilwell took over the U.S. Tenth Army in June 1945 during the bloody struggle for Okinawa; he replaced Lieutenant General Simon B. Buckner, who had been killed in action. During the war Stilwell's heart had been in his efforts to reform Chiang's army, but the Nationalist forces in China seemed to him, even before he left Asia, to be obsolete, corrupt, and doomed. As his biographer observed, "China was a problem for which there was no American solution.... In the end China went her own way as if the Americans had never come."

13

MacArthur's Final Campaigns

THE STRATEGIC ISSUE in the Pacific that most occupied the Joint Chiefs in 1944 was whether Luzon, Formosa, or Fukien was the best site to seize for the staging of final operations against Japan. General Arnold still believed in the efficacy of strategic bombing as a war-winning weapon in its own right, and Admiral King continued to maintain that the Pacific Fleet could force Japan's capitulation through blockade, air and sea bombardments, and mine laying. Growing Japanese resistance in the island campaigns, however, pointed toward the probable need for a ground invasion of Japan. The War and Navy departments began to develop contingency plans for using the army and marines. King was known for his persistent opposition to retaking the Philippines as too expensive and time-consuming. He favored either the invasion of Formosa or of the Amoy area of Fukien province, on the Chinese mainland west of Formosa. By late spring 1944 Marshall and Arnold were turning away from MacArthur's insistence on taking Luzon because that advance seemed likely to require enormous human and materiel resources.

In a conference at Pearl Harbor in July, Roosevelt and Leahy, the JCS chairman, appeared to be more persuaded by MacArthur's arguments for the Luzon route than by Nimitz's case for an invasion of Formosa. The Fukien option had been eliminated by the great Japanese offensive that was sweeping across large areas of China west of the Amoy region. King did not immediately yield, however, and the Joint Chiefs kept the Luzon-versus-Formosa debate alive until October 2 when King and Nimitz agreed that they could not logistically mount a Formosa assault in the near future. Forthwith the JCS sent a directive to MacArthur authorizing his invasion of Luzon. He already had approval to attack the Philippines, but his assault target had been limited to Mindanao and then changed in September to Leyte.

The JCS and MacArthur had agreed on October 20 as the invasion day at Leyte. More than 200,000 troops of Krueger's Sixth Army were to be committed to the four-beach assault on the east side of the island. Barbey's VII Amphibious Force would transport the troops, with fire support provided by Kinkaid's Seventh Fleet, Halsey's Third Fleet, and Kenney's Allied Air Forces of the Southwest Pacific Area, notably the U.S. Fifth Air Force, now led by Lieutenant General Ennis P. Whitehead.

When the first American soldiers went ashore on Leyte, they were surprised by the moderate to light opposition. Actually, the enemy had only 23,000 troops on the island. Eventually, Lieutenant General Sosaku Suzuki, commander of the Japanese Thirty-fifth Army and head of defenses south of Luzon, deployed another 50,000 soldiers to Leyte. Meanwhile, Sixth Army strength there was built up to 258,000 men.

MacArthur, who had arrived on a cruiser in Leyte Gulf, went ashore the first day and the following three to visit the four beachheads. He moved his advance headquarters to Tacloban, the island's principal city, soon after its capture on the 21st. Tacloban was hit by more than thirty enemy air raids during the final week of October, but MacArthur escaped injury.

The Japanese high command immediately set in motion several projects to prevent MacArthur's forces from capturing Leyte. More troops were rushed down from Luzon, and massive air strikes were mounted against the seven hundred

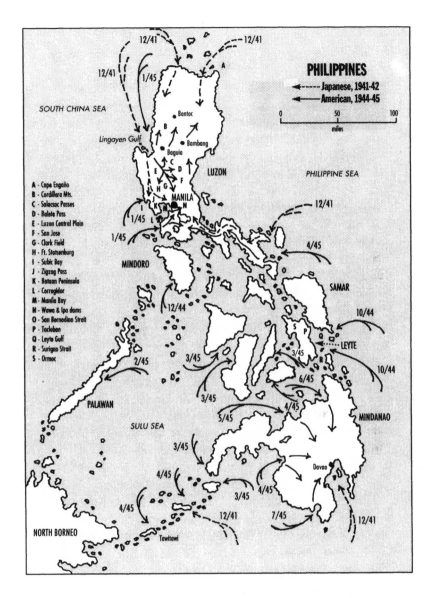

PHILIPPINES

- - - ◄ Japanese, 1941-42
——◄ American, 1944-45

0   50   100
miles

SOUTH CHINA SEA

12/41
12/41
12/41
1/45

Bontoc

Lingayen Gulf

Baguio
Bambang

LUZON

PHILIPPINE SEA

A - Cape Engaño
B - Cordillera Mts.
C - Salacsac Passes
D - Balete Pass
E - Luzon Central Plain
F - San Jose
G - Clark Field
H - Ft. Stotsenburg
I - Subic Bay
J - Zigzag Pass
K - Bataan Peninsula
L - Corregidor
M - Manila Bay
N - Wawa & Ipo dams
O - San Bernadino Strait
P - Tacloban
Q - Leyte Gulf
R - Surigao Strait
S - Ormoc

MANILA

1/45

1/45

MINDORO

12/44

12/41

4/45

SAMAR

10/44

LEYTE

10/44

3/45
3/45
6/45
4/45
5/45

2/45

3/45

3/45

PALAWAN

SULU SEA

MINDANAO

3/45

4/45

4/45

Davao

4/45

NORTH BORNEO

Tawitawi

4/45

12/41

3/45

7/45

12/41

ships in Leyte Gulf. The first kamikazes (suicidal air missions) of the war were deployed against American combat and merchant vessels off Leyte with deadly results. The most important Japanese reaction was the commitment of the Combined Fleet that resulted in the battle for Leyte

Gulf, October 23–25. This was the largest naval engagement in history and marked the virtual end of the Japanese navy.

The Japanese Northern Force, made up largely of carriers without aircraft, acted as a successful decoy in luring Halsey's Third Fleet northward away from Leyte. The force was decimated, however, by Halsey's planes off Cape Engaño, Luzon, on October 25. Meanwhile, the Japanese Southern Force and Fifth Fleet tried to break through the Surigao Strait into Leyte Gulf on October 24–25. Both enemy fleets were almost wiped out in the strait by the U.S. Seventh Fleet, which included some of the old battleships that had been hit in the 1941 Pearl Harbor attack.

The most powerful of the four Japanese fleets was Vice Admiral Takeo Kurita's Central Force. In a running battle with American submarines and planes in Central Philippine waters, October 23–24, the Central Force lost its super battleship and two cruisers. With Halsey's fleet far off to the north, Kurita's still formidable force passed through the strait between Luzon and Samar and turned south toward the entrance to Leyte Gulf. Kurita surprised a group of escort carriers and destroyers commanded by Rear Admiral Clifton A. F. Sprague off the southeastern tip of Samar, only a short distance from the hundreds of vulnerable American transports and cargo ships anchored off the Leyte beachheads. Sprague's small force put up a gallant fight but was in danger of annihilation when Kurita suddenly broke off the action and retreated. A number of his ships were sunk by U.S. aircraft and submarines as they tried to leave Philippine waters. Thus were spared not only Sprague's ships and the noncombatants off Leyte but also the main supply stores for the Sixth Army.

The American navy lost six ships in the battle for Leyte Gulf; the Japanese naval losses were horrendous—four carriers, three battleships, ten cruisers, and nine destroyers. It was to be the last surface battle for the Japanese Combined Fleet.

While these momentous naval actions erupted in the seas around Leyte, Krueger's Sixth Army divisions seized the eastern half of the island, cut the enemy forces in two by advancing to the west coast, and even captured the western part of nearby Samar Island. By November the bulk of Suzuki's much-reinforced Thirty-fifth Army was well entrenched in the mountains of northwestern Leyte. The fighting grew heavier as Krueger's soldiers, also strongly reinforced, tried to penetrate the final redoubts of the surrounded enemy forces. In a surprise amphibious assault on December 7, American troops took Ormoc, the last enemy-held port on Leyte. Suzuki's soldiers fought on stubbornly in the mountainous region, though General Tomoyuki Yamashita, overall commander in the Philippines, informed him on December 19 that no further reinforcements would be sent to Leyte because the defense was now considered hopeless.

Seven days later MacArthur prematurely announced, "The Leyte-Samar campaign can now be regarded as closed except for minor mopping-up." That day he ordered Eichelberger's recently established Eighth Army to begin relieving the Sixth Army on Leyte. The Eighth Army's portion of the campaign was not finished until early May, by which time 700 of Eichelberger's men had been killed and 27,000 more Japanese had died in action. Altogether, American casualties for the entire Leyte-Samar campaign totaled 16,000 compared with 73,000 Japanese, most of the latter killed in action. Suzuki died in April 1945 when American aircraft sank the ship on which he was trying to escape.

The campaign on Leyte had been disappointingly long and costly for the Americans. MacArthur and Kenney were especially upset to find that, according to engineers, the island's soil was not suitable for bomber bases. The inability to exploit Leyte for air support in the Luzon invasion reinforced MacArthur's belief that air bases would have to be established on Mindoro, south of Manila Bay. On December 15 two of Krueger's regiments seized the island against light resistance. Air bases were hastily built on Mindoro and did prove important in providing land-based air strength to supplement carrier planes in supporting the invasion of Luzon.

The climax of the Southwest Pacific war was the liberation of the island of Luzon, the site of Manila and a large proportion of the population, as well as industrial and maritime activity, in the Philippines. MacArthur was eager to reopen Manila Bay, the best harbor in his theater, and to take on the vaunted Yamashita, conqueror of Singapore. But the Southwest Pacific commander was motivated also by deeply emotional personal ties to Manila. It had been his home from 1935 to 1941, as well as on three earlier tours of duty in the Philippines, during which he had cultivated close friendships with a number of powerful Filipino politicians and entrepreneurs. For him, the whole advance from Buna to Luzon had been a move he was destined to make. Sometimes the return to the Philippines became an overwhelming obsession for MacArthur, a way of redeeming himself after the loss of the islands in 1941–1942; in other moments he saw it as a sentimental journey back to his second home.

Krueger's Sixth Army, which MacArthur had entrusted with spearheading the American offensives in the Southwest Pacific so far, was assigned the main role in the liberation of Luzon, with several units of the Eighth Army attached. Both carrier and land-based air support was plentiful, supplied by Whitehead's Fifth Air Force and the carriers of Halsey's Third and Kinkaid's Seventh Fleets. Barbey's VII Amphibious Force, as usual, was to handle the transport and amphibious phases. Altogether, Barbey would direct fifty-six amphibious assaults during the war—far more than any other amphibious force commander. With one thousand ships used in the invasion, the Luzon assault was the largest of the war against Japan. As the army's official history attests, the Luzon campaign from January 9, 1945, to the end of the war on August 15 "entailed the use of more U.S. Army ground combat and service forces than did operations in North Africa, Italy, or southern France and was larger than the entire Allied commitment to Sicily."

It was well that the Americans came in strength, for awaiting them was General Yamashita's Fourteenth Area Army, made up of three armies cleverly located in mountain bastions in North, East, and West Luzon. Yamashita's own Shobu Group of 152,000 soldiers was in the mountains north of the Luzon Central Plain; the Shimbu Group of 80,000 troops was located in rugged country east of Manila; and the Kembu Group of 30,000 men was situated around Clark Field and the nearby mountains to the west. Yamashita intended to yield the Central Plain and Manila without major battles, but Rear Admiral Rikichi Iwabuchi, who headed the Manila Naval Defense Force, along with some Shimbu troops who did not make it into the mountains before the city was encircled, did not recognize Yamashita's authority and insubordinately chose to fight to the death with his 21,000 men in Manila.

During the Mindoro and Luzon invasions, kamikazes made life nightmarish for the men aboard American ships. Between December 13 and January 13, Japanese aircraft, mostly kamikazes, sank twenty-four ships and damaged sixty-seven others in those two invasion armadas, resulting in four thousand American casualties. These frantic efforts cost the enemy six hundred aircraft, virtually eliminating Japanese air power in the Philippines. The Luzon invasion force was also attacked by Japanese midget submarines, with several torpedoes narrowly missing the cruiser that carried MacArthur and several of his senior commanders.

After a week of naval and air attacks, Krueger's Sixth Army began landing on January 9, 1945, along the shores of Lingayen Gulf, on the northwest coast of Luzon where Homma's army had landed in December 1941. The beaches were lightly defended, and Krueger's men were able to move south into the Central Plain. The Japanese savagely resisted the two American corps leading the offensive, especially around the old American bases of Fort Stotsenburg and Clark Field, which were finally taken at the end of January. To the east across the Central Plain, Sixth Army troops fought a long, intense battle against Yamashita's only armored division. The battle of San Jose ended on February 8 in a decisive American victory over the Japanese division, which was built around a nucleus of several hundred tanks; nearly all the enemy troops and vehicles were destroyed.

Meanwhile, southwest of Clark Field, Hall's XI Corps made an amphibious assault on January 29 near Subic Bay, site of an old American naval base. His units pushed rapidly eastward until abruptly halted by strong enemy fire in the mountains above the northwest corner of Bataan Peninsula. In the battle of Zigzag Pass, elements of the Kembu Group stopped the American advance until mid-February when they were eliminated. American troops then proceeded to take Bataan easily. Yamashita had decided not to duplicate MacArthur's move of the winter of 1941–1942 in sending large forces into the disease-ridden peninsula where they could be trapped. By early March, Sixth Army forces battling the Kembu Group had largely destroyed it as an effective army.

MacArthur dispatched three divisions in a race to Manila, with an infantry division and a cavalry division descending on the Philippine capital from the north and an airborne division from the south. The airborne unit was part of Eichelberger's Eighth Army while the other two divisions were in Lieutenant General Oscar W. Griswold's XIV Corps of Krueger's Sixth Army. MacArthur gave Griswold command of all the forces involved in the battle to liberate Manila. The cavalrymen won the race to Manila, soon followed by the infantry. By February 7 the area of the city north of the Pasig River, which runs through the middle, was largely cleared of Japanese troops, with the fighting less fierce than expected. Griswold's men freed thousands of American, Allied, and Filipino prisoners of war and civilian internees, nearly all in badly emaciated condition, at several large prisons on the north side of the Pasig. MacArthur, who was north of Manila at the time, misjudged the opposition still ahead and prematurely announced on February 6 that the Japanese defenders' "complete destruction is imminent." The city was finally liberated almost a month later, on March 4, after the only large urban battle of the Pacific war. American forces lost 1,000 dead and 5,600 wounded in the hard-fought struggle for Manila. Iwabuchi died in action with 16,000 of his men; about 5,000 escaped to the Shimbu Group; only a small number of the Manila defenders were taken prisoner. One hundred thousand or more Filipino civilians lost their lives during the battle. Many were killed inadvertently by combat fire, particularly artillery, but 60,000 were slain in atrocities by Japanese soldiers in the final days. Some authorities who visited postwar Dresden, Warsaw, and Stalingrad maintained that the material destruction of Manila was worse. So desperate were the devastated city's needs that it became more a liability than an asset in prosecuting the campaign on Luzon. MacArthur had to divert considerable troops, equipment, and supplies for emergency relief and rehabilitation.

During the fighting in Manila, MacArthur assigned Hall's XI Corps the job of clearing the entrance to Manila Bay, namely, Bataan and the islands at the bay entrance, chief of which was Corregidor. Because American intelligence showed only an 850-man enemy garrison on Corregidor, the American force of 3,000 airborne and infantry troops was more than surprised to find itself outnumbered by a 5,200-man Japanese force. The Americans were fortunate that the enemy soldiers were scattered, with poor communication between units, and that massive support by American naval and air power was effective. Organized resistance on the island ended in two weeks, on March 1. Many of the Japanese in underground tunnels, as well as Americans above ground, died in numerous great explosions set off deliberately by the enemy. It was a bizarre but fierce battle to the end. Only 20 Japanese were captured, the rest killed, while American casualties were 220 dead or missing and 790 wounded.

In April, American forces recaptured two nearby islands

just south of Corregidor, thus clearing the bay entrance. Because of hundreds of mines and three hundred sunken ships, Manila harbor was not usable until early May.

With the end of the battle of Manila, Krueger moved two corps of his army into action east of the city against the Shimbu Group. The Japanese were in excellent defensive positions in the mountains, and they made the Americans' progress slow and expensive; two American division commanders became casualties in the spring operations against the Shimbu defenders. The largest battles were for Wawa and Ipo dams, situated in high country; the seizure of them was essential to gain control of Manila's water supply. The battle for Wawa Dam involved four American divisions and lasted three months, until May 28 when the Americans secured the area. The savage fight for Ipo Dam began May 6 and ended twelve days later in an American victory. In the Ipo battle seven hundred American planes dropped napalm bombs on Japanese positions in a massive attack before the final American assault. The Shimbu Group was finished as a potent fighting force by early June, but six thousand remnants resisted in scattered pockets in the mountains until the end of the war.

The Sixth Army's longest, largest, and costliest operations by far were those against Yamashita's strongest army, the Shobu Group, which he personally commanded in the mountains of Northwest Luzon. The campaign lasted more than six months and involved simultaneous heavy combat on three fronts—in the areas of Baguio, Bambang, and Bontoc. Filipino guerrilla forces, often led by American veterans of the Bataan campaign, were valuable in all three areas of large-scale combat. Among numerous division-level battles, some drew in more forces before the outcome was decided. The battle of the Salacsac Passes, which lasted almost three months, and the fight for Balete Pass, which also went on from March to May, are among the largest and bloodiest of the mostly unknown clashes on Krueger's long front against Yamashita's army. When Japan surrendered in mid-August, Sixth Army forces and Filipino guerrillas had surrounded Yamashita in the Bontoc area high in the Cordillera Central Mountains of northwestern Luzon. After learning of the surrender, the Japanese, still full of fight and numbering more than fifty thousand soldiers, followed Yamashita out of their defense lines and laid down their arms to the Sixth Army.

Yamashita's Fourteenth Area Army suffered 205,000 troops killed in the Luzon campaign, in addition to 16,000 Japanese who died in the Manila battle. American ground forces lost 8,200 killed, 32,700 wounded, and 93,400 noncombat casualties (mainly disease). The Filipino-American guerrillas lost 1,100 dead and 6,200 wounded. In terms of American ground forces killed in action, the Luzon campaign exacted the highest toll of the Pacific War. Yamashita's armies had fought the most effective operations of delay and attrition on Luzon.

Months before the Leyte invasion, MacArthur had proposed the seizure of the rest of the southern Philippines, but the Joint Chiefs had rejected it as strategically unnecessary. Nevertheless, in February 1945, while the Sixth Army was heavily engaged on Luzon and elements of the Eighth Army were pursuing Suzuki's remaining forces on Leyte, MacArthur ordered Eichelberger to commit the bulk of his Eighth Army in a lightninglike series of amphibious assaults in the southern islands. Eight of the eleven major amphibious operations in the archipelago after the invasion of Luzon were undertaken on MacArthur's orders before he received authorization from the Joint Chiefs. The 68,000 Japanese troops in the southern Philippines were scattered in small garrisons, except for the well-organized defenses on eastern Mindanao.

The first of Eichelberger's southern assaults was against Palawan in late February. The next month Eighth Army units invaded six more islands in the southern Philippines and took them rapidly. In April American troops landed on three others that were lightly held and then collided with enemy strength on Mindanao, where three further amphibious assaults were necessary. Davao, the principal city of Mindanao, was taken on May 3. The conquest of eastern Mindanao took about six weeks and involved two infantry divisions and two regimental combat teams of Eichelberger's army against 56,000 tenacious Japanese defenders. Some enemy pockets in the mountainous interior were still resisting at the end of the war.

The Eighth Army's casualties in the southern Philippines amounted to 2,100 men killed and 7,000 wounded, while 28,000 Japanese were killed and several hundred were taken prisoner. Nearly 40,000 Japanese troops surrendered in the southern islands after the cessation of hostilities. A high proportion of the casualties on both sides in the southern operations occurred on eastern Mindanao.

MacArthur's tangential strategy in the spring and summer of 1945 sent other forces southward. In addition to Eichelberger's Eighth Army operations in the southern Philippines, elements of the Australian First Army, on MacArthur's orders, had been engaged for some time in mopping up isolated enemy units on Bougainville, New Britain, and Northeast New Guinea.

Beginning in May 1945 MacArthur sent the Australian I Corps to retake three oil centers along the coasts of Borneo. The Aussies were supported strongly by the American Fifth Air Force, Seventh Fleet, and VII Amphibious Force. The Australians landed on Tarakan Island off the northeast coast of Borneo on May 1, securing the island after an expensive seven-week struggle. Next, on June 10, Australian troops conducted an amphibious assault at Brunei Bay, on the west side of Borneo. Also involving fierce combat, this operation took three weeks. The last of these ventures was an amphibious landing at Balikpapan on July 1. The Australians fought for three weeks before securing the area.

The Joint Chiefs had reluctantly approved the Borneo operations, mainly because they were convinced that the damaged oil fields and facilities could not be readied for production again before the war ended. If MacArthur had continued to commit his forces on tangents south of Luzon, it might have been difficult for him to mount Operation Olympic, the assault on Kyushu, Japan, set for that November. Fortunately, Japan's sudden surrender made moot the questions of his forces' readiness for an invasion of Japan and the Philippines' preparedness as a staging base for that grand assault.

14

Climax in the Central Pacific

ONCE THE B-29 bombing campaign began against Japan from the Marianas in the autumn of 1944, it was almost inevitable that the United States would undertake the conquest of all or part of the Volcano and Bonin islands, situated halfway between the Marianas and Japan. In October the JCS directed Nimitz to seize Iwo Jima, an eight-square-mile island covered with volcanic ash in the appropriately named Volcano Islands. Intelligence indicated that, of all the Volcano-Bonin group, Iwo Jima has terrain best suited for air bases. Indeed, it already had two Japanese bases and another under construction; enemy aircraft from there had been attacking B-29s, which at that time were flying to and from Japan without fighter escorts. In American hands, the island could provide bases for both fighters and medium bombers within range of the enemy home islands, for air-sea rescue operations in case of ditched planes or ship crews in trouble, and particularly for emergency stops by B-29s that were damaged or needed fuel.

The Japanese high command also viewed Iwo Jima as a likely American objective for most of the same reasons. Lieutenant General Tadamachi Kuribayashi, a highly competent commander, was sent there with reinforcements that brought the garrison to 21,000 soldiers, including 7,000 naval troops. The Japanese built hundreds of pillboxes and other fortifications, providing coordinated fire coverage of the beaches and linked by extensive tunnels. The dominant terrain feature, Mount Suribachi, on the island's southern tip, was transformed into a bristling fortress, while on the northern end of the island a rugged lava plateau with steep hills and ravines was loaded with concealed gun positions and underground shelters. Kuribayashi expected the invaders to come ashore at the low waist of the island where every square yard was covered by the multitude of machine guns, mortars, and field artillery pieces installed on Suribachi or the northern plateau. Anticipating a thorough pre-assault bombardment, Kuribayashi sheltered his principal gun emplacements so well that only direct hits by large shells or bombs would cause serious damage.

Land-based B-24s from the Marianas had been bombing Iwo Harbor daily for over two months, and the Japanese garrison had suffered through five naval bombardments during that span. In view of the small size of the island, Central Pacific planners thought three days of pre-assault bombardment by aircraft and surface ships would suffice. When the preparatory attacks began, Mitscher's Fast Carrier Force, with Spruance aboard, was off on a two-day raid of the Tokyo area, the first since Doolittle's in April 1942 and far more devastating. Meanwhile, Turner's Amphibious Support Force of battleships and cruisers began firing at known and suspected targets on Iwo Jima on February 16, 1945. The Fast Carrier Force arrived from the waters off Japan in time to deliver air attacks during the final phase of the bombardment before the troops went ashore.

The surface ships and carrier aircraft again shelled, bombed, and strafed for nearly two hours before the first troops of two marine divisions began landing at 9 a.m. on February 19. In spite of "the heaviest prelanding bombardment of the war," the invaders soon found themselves under fire from all directions, as if all the earlier "softening up" had not seriously affected the enemy's ability to respond. Actually, many of the Japanese had remained in underground shelters during the intense earlier bombardment that morning.

Admiral Hill's Attack Force transported the marines to the island, where General Schmidt, head of the V Amphibious Corps, assumed command ashore. Two colorful and critical observers were General Holland Smith of Fleet Marine Force, Pacific, and James V. Forrestal, the new secretary of the navy.

The deep volcanic ash of the shoreline presented difficulties that had not been anticipated: the tracks of the amphibious landing vehicles sank into the soft ash without gripping well, while conventional landing craft often had trouble beaching and were swamped. The mounting wreckage of damaged craft along the beaches caused problems in navigating later incoming vessels to the shore and led to collisions. The chaos at the beaches resulted in late arrivals of heavy weapons and tanks. The heavily laden marines, moreover, had to climb a series of terraces to reach the central sector of the island; they were slowed not only by heavy enemy fire but also by the ash, which was much harder to walk in than sand. The marines ashore found little vegetation or terrain indentations in which to hide from enemy fire.

Nevertheless, they generally got off the beaches the first day. Troops on the left flank pushed across the waist of the island, cutting off the Mount Suribachi defenders from the rest of the garrison, and marines in the middle drove inland as far as one of the air bases. On the right flank, however, the men suffered through the most intense fire of the day, which came from the plateau on the north end; they were unable to get off the beaches on the 19th. More than 2,400 marines became casualties the first day on Iwo Jima.

The next day the Americans in the center seized the air base in their sector. The troops to their left began the assault on Suribachi, and the marines to their right started up the plateau from the beaches. The climax of the three-day battle for Mount Suribachi was the raising of the American flag atop the 550-foot volcano. A photograph of the reenactment of the flag-raising later that day became perhaps the best-known picture of American forces in action in World

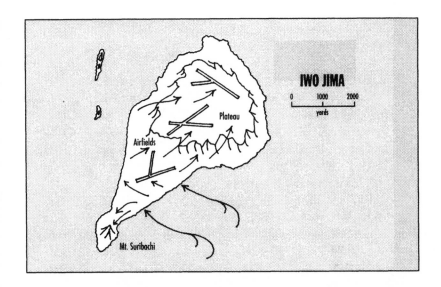

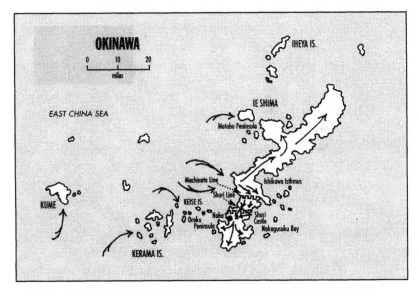

War II. After the capture of the Suribachi stronghold, the
marine division that had been in reserve came ashore and
took the center of the line as the other two divisions turned
north toward the plateau. By then large amounts of American heavy weapons were available on the island to support

the marines' advance, together with excellent fire support from the ships offshore. Despite such heavy barrages, many of the enemy's defensive positions were so well sheltered that the marines still had to cope with them individually, using satchel demolitions, grenades, flamethrowers, and tanks.

Japanese aircraft, including kamikazes, attacked on February 21, the suicide planes doing the main damage. Kamikazes collided with five ships, sinking one carrier and severely damaging another.

The fighting was sometimes hand to hand and always intense with more than 80,000 men locked in battle on the small island. It continued until Iwo Jima was finally secured on March 16 after thirty-six days of desperate combat; American planners had predicted the operation would be concluded in less than a week. On March 26 the hell began again briefly when 260 Japanese who had hidden underground emerged and launched several attacks before being eliminated. Altogether the Japanese lost 20,900 dead and 1,100 captured. Almost 26,000 Americans became casualties, including 6,800 killed or missing. The battle for Iwo Jima was the fourth costliest of the Pacific war for Americans, and it was the only one where American casualties outnumbered the enemy's.

Was it worth the sacrifice? Arguably, yes. Between 25,000 and 27,000 crewmen of the U.S. army air forces were saved by air-sea rescue missions from Iwo Jima; 2,250 emergency landings were made there by B-29s returning from raids on Japan. By early April, fighters from the island started escorting the B-29s, increasing the bombers' effectiveness and protecting an inestimable number of crewmen's lives. Had the invasion of Japan been mounted in the fall of 1945, Iwo Jima undoubtedly would have served other functions in saving more American boys, including support missions for the invaders of Kyushu.

When the Joint Chiefs in October 1944 authorized Nimitz to seize Iwo Jima, they also directed him to capture Okinawa next. The strategic importance of Okinawa to both

American and Japanese planners was based on its proximity to Japan—it was only 350 miles south of Kyushu. There was no doubt at Nimitz's headquarters that a thrust into this largest island of the Ryukyu Archipelago, between Formosa and Kyushu, would be viewed in Tokyo as an advance into Japan's inner defense system and would be met with as powerful a defensive response as could be mounted.

Nimitz's plan called for a preliminary move into the small Kerama and Keise islands off the southwest corner of Okinawa and for an assault on Ie Shima, an island off the west coast, farther north, that contained a Japanese air base. Okinawa itself is over 450 square miles in size and has three distinctive terrain regions. The southern end of the island provides, as a U.S. marine historian observes, "an ideal natural defense against an enemy moving down from the north," being full of hills and rugged plateaus; the middle area, extending from the capital city of Naha on the south-west coast to the narrow Ishikawa Isthmus, has a good terrain setting of high cliffs and deep valleys for defensive works extending west of the ancient landmark of Shuri Castle; and the northern area of the island is characterized by piney woods and mountains. Two-thirds of the island is situated north of the Ishikawa Isthmus, but the Japanese wisely chose to concentrate their firepower in the southern region.

Lieutenant General Mitsuru Ushijima's Thirty-second Army of 115,000 men was stationed on Okinawa. The defenders had a larger quantity of heavy weapons than any other enemy garrison the Americans encountered in the Pacific War. They included three hundred howitzers and artillery pieces of 70 mm or higher caliber, including sixty-four 150 mm guns, and a large number of excellent 47 mm antitank guns. The Okinawa forces could also count on strong air support, with dozens of Japanese air bases within range on Formosa, the China coast, the northern Ryukyus, and Kyushu.

Although Central Pacific intelligence estimated the Japanese troop strength on Okinawa at only half its actual number, Nimitz, as POA theater commander, was able to draw upon enormous ground, sea, and air resources: more than twelve hundred ships, excluding Mitscher's Fast Carrier Force; 183,000 combat troops and 115,000 service troops; and thousands of carrier and land-based aircraft. Spruance, the Fifth Fleet head, was in overall charge of the huge Okinawa campaign, designated Operation Iceberg. Under him, the top command echelon consisted of Admiral Turner, heading the Joint Expeditionary Force, and army General Simon Buckner, commander of the Tenth Army, which comprised marine General Geiger's III Amphibious Corps of three marine divisions and one army, and Major General John R. Hodge's XXIV Corps of four infantry divisions. The army air power that was committed came from the Fifth, Thirteenth, Seventh, and even the Twentieth air forces, which in mid-March began attacking enemy air and naval bases from southern Japan to Formosa and the China coast. Japan's Inland Sea and other waters off Japan were heavily mined to deter the remaining Japanese ships from sailing to Okinawa.

U.S. army soldiers easily captured the offshore Kerama and Keise islands during the week before the main Okinawa assault, set for April 1. The principal invasion, along the southwest coast, was preceded by extensive underwater demolition work at night on the targeted shoreline, along with heavy preparatory bombardments by planes and ships. Two marine divisions on the north and two army divisions on the south made up the first forces ashore. At the end of the first day the Americans held a beachhead nine miles long and three miles deep. Enemy ground opposition had been surprisingly light, though kamikazes quickly began attacking the huge number of ships lying offshore.

Within three days the beachhead had been enlarged to double its first-day size, and two enemy airfields had been captured. Some of the invaders nourished the illusion of a quick operation, but Ushijima had deliberately withdrawn his main forces from the beaches into powerful defensive works to the south, which the Americans would not encounter for some days. The island was cut at its waist during the first several days, with Geiger's III Amphibious Corps then undertaking the reduction of the northern region and Hodge's XXIV Corps moving slowly south against growing resistance. Motobu Peninsula on the west coast was secured on April 12 by the marines, who a week later overran the rest of the northern two-thirds of the islands, though some mopping up remained.

Meanwhile, army forces assaulted Ie Shima, off the west coast, on April 16. The seven-thousand-man garrison put up a hard five-day fight before succumbing. Losses were heavy on both sides, with Ernie Pyle, the famed correspondent, being one of those killed. During the same period, army and marine units on the eastern side of Okinawa took several islands that enabled American shipping to begin entering Nakagusuku Bay (later renamed Buckner Bay) and that led to the installation of offshore radar stations that would help warn the ships of incoming kamikazes.

Beginning on April 6, kamikaze attacks had increased markedly, both against the beachhead and vessels offshore. On that day alone, 135 kamikazes were destroyed while the suicidal and conventional enemy air missions sank 6 American ships. By the end of the month the toll of kamikaze victims had risen to 20 ships sunk and 147 damaged. More than 1,900 kamikazes were sent to the Okinawa area before the campaign ended, resulting in the U.S. navy's greatest losses of the war: 36 ships sunk, 368 vessels damaged, and 760 aircraft destroyed. The British Royal Navy, which contributed a small fleet for the Okinawa operation, also fell prey to kamikazes. The picket ships, usually destroyers, caught many of the kamikaze attacks; one American destroyer somehow survived direct hits by six kamikazes. Ever since the initial attacks at Leyte Gulf in October 1944, American forces had been trying to devise ways of countering kamikazes, but no certain protection against these deadly attackers was developed before the capitulation of Japan.

The climactic fighting on Okinawa was set off when Hodge's army forces attacked the enemy's Machinato Line, one of several strongly fortified positions in the rough country around Shuri Castle on the southern front. The fierce Japanese reaction surprised the attackers; American intelligence had not discovered the fortifications in advance. The three-division assault ended in bloody repulses for the Americans in all sectors; they suffered more than seven hundred casualties the first day. The Machinato Line was not penetrated for another five days of severe combat, and even then the Japanese stubbornly clung to both ends of the defensive line, yielding only in the middle. By May 1 two of the army divisions were so exhausted and battered that they had to be relieved by a marine and an army division. The move was timely, for three days later Ushijima launched intense artillery barrages and infantry counterattacks all along the line, besides attempting an amphibious assault behind the American lines that was defeated. The Japanese achieved penetrations in several places along the main front before being thrown back; the counterattacks cost six thousand Japanese dead.

Thereafter Ushijima turned mainly to defensive tactics, delaying the American conquest as long as possible and making the invaders pay horribly in casualties. His fortifications were centered on the city of Naha and the inner defensive rings around Shuri Castle. Buckner reorganized his order of advance after Ushijima's wild counterattacks, replacing some casualty-ridden units and bringing in troop reinforcements and more tactical air and artillery support. By May 10 five American divisions held the frontline: two marine divisions in the Naha sector and northwest of Shuri Castle, and three army divisions east of Shuri and along the east coast.

Buckner began an offensive all along the front the next day, but the defenders on the Shuri Line were well armed, tenacious, and positioned in strong, cleverly hidden fortifications. One authority claims with good justification that the

Shuri Line "was probably the strongest position the Americans had encountered in the Pacific war." The defensive works included many caves with connecting underground corridors, well-built pillboxes and blockhouses, mutually supporting strongpoints, and even thick stone burial shrines that had been well fortified.

Heavy rains paralyzed American tanks and mechanized vehicles during the first week of Buckner's end-the-campaign offensive in May. The Japanese did not retreat southward from the Shuri Line until the 19th, after an infantry division captured a key hill position that could have led to an envelopment of Ushijima's positions. The marines seized Naha after a hard battle on May 29 and then captured Shuri Castle. Relief was not in sight, the Americans could tell, because the enemy's withdrawal was a fighting one, with the troops showing good discipline, order, and high spirits.

In June the battlefields were principally on the Oroku Peninsula, southwest of Naha, and along a line of ridges and hills spanning the southern tip of Okinawa. A marine division crossed the harbor at Naha and landed on the Oroku Peninsula on June 4, while another marine division began driving across the base of the peninsula to entrap the Japanese there. Rugged terrain, rainy weather, and fierce opposition slowed the marine advances; Oroku Peninsula was not secured for eleven days.

Other marine and army troops pushed slowly but steadily through the rugged terrain at the island's southern tip, which contained its highest hills. This was Ushijima's final defensive line, and his men fought frantically and stubbornly. The eastern end of the line began to collapse on June 12 under overwhelming American firepower, but the Japanese on two key ridges to the west held back the efforts of three American divisions until the 17th, when the last line gave way. The remaining troops were scattered along the southern coast. Geiger declared Okinawa secured on June 22, but a disappointing amount of fighting continued for a week in the mopping-up phase.

In contrast to the tragedy at the end of the Saipan battle, an unprecedented number of Japanese troops surrendered: 7,400. This is attributed to an effective American psychological warfare program of broadcasts and leaflets that had been developed since Saipan. All sides on Okinawa lost heavily in the long, enormous struggle: 110,000 Japanese troops dead; 42,000 Okinawa civilian casualties; and nearly 50,000 American combat casualties. The marine and army divisions of the U.S. Tenth Army lost 7,600 killed or missing and 31,800 wounded, along with 26,200 noncombatant casualties. Besides 4,800 sailors wounded, the American navy lost 4,900 men killed or missing in action, so devastating had been the kamikaze raids. Both ground commanders died during the campaign: Buckner was killed on June 18 by an artillery shell, and Ushijima took his own life four days later. General Stilwell succeeded Buckner for the final days of the fighting.

After the battle, American construction projects were rapidly set in motion to prepare facilities for the staging of the invasion of Kyushu in November. The only B-29 mission from Okinawa against Japan came on the last night of the war. Thus the island that had precipitated the bloodiest battle of the Pacific conflict never served as a staging base for an assault on Japan, and its B-29 airfield was used but once for a mission.

Indirectly, nevertheless, the Okinawa campaign was not fought in vain: it was a factor in Truman's decision to drop atomic bombs on Japan. The capture of Okinawa had been so costly for the Americans that the president wished to avert another large-scale ground operation against the increasingly fanatical Japanese. Truman concluded that the only way to avoid an invasion of Japan was to use the atomic bombs in a bid quickly to end the war.

15

Avenues to Surrender

FOR MANY MONTHS before Japan's sudden capitulation on August 15, 1945, the Joint Chiefs of Staff and their planners pondered the efficacy of naval blockade, strategic bombing, or massive invasion as the wisest way to compel Japan to surrender. The first two of these were among the most devastating campaigns of the Pacific war and lent credence to the case for a strategy of attrition. Detailed plans were also developed, however, for the invasions of the Japanese home islands that many leaders feared would be incredibly costly but also inevitable.

While the Japanese employed their submarines mainly against warships and to transport supplies and troops, the American navy directed its submarine campaign primarily against merchant shipping and Japan's lines of communications to its Southern Resources Area (Southeast Asia) and the Asian mainland. The submarines of the Pacific Fleet also were extremely effective against enemy combat vessels, but their destruction of Japan's merchantmen and thus her links to strategic natural resources was far more significant in the long run. If Japanese submarines had been employed in the ways American underseas craft were used, they might have seriously handicapped Allied logistical efforts in the Pacific.

Submarines and long-range bombers were the best weapons for penetrating Japan's overextended empire. The Pacific conflict evolved into a war of distances, especially when contrasted with the struggle in Europe. The width of the southern reaches of the Japanese Empire at its maximum was 6,400 miles, while its north-south extremities were 5,300 miles apart. Batavia, Java, which lay in the heart of Japan's principal sources of raw materials, lay 4,100 miles south of Tokyo. The oceanic perimeter of the Japanese expansion at its height was 14,200 miles long, equivalent to over half the earth's circumference. Shipping was the linchpin that made possible Japan's control of the natural resources region on which it depended; it was also the key to supplying its far-flung bases, ranging from the Aleutians to the Solomons to Burma.

Large numbers of long-range submarines with effective torpedoes was the logical way to cut Japan's long arteries of supply with her distant imperial possessions. Until late 1943, however, the Pacific Fleet's submarine force, skillfully led by Vice Admiral Charles A. Lockwood through the latter part of the war, did not have an adequate quantity of fleet submarines with distant-cruise capabilities, and early on the torpedoes were woefully defective. For instance, Admiral Thomas C. Hart, head of the small U.S. Asiatic Fleet stationed in the Philippines at the start of the war, had one supposedly major asset—twenty-eight submarines—but nearly all of them had proved of little value in attacking the many enemy ships involved in the Philippine invasion or in the busy shipping channels of the South China Sea. Lockwood himself contributed to torpedo improvement when he was a submarine captain by coolly lying off Truk and firing fifteen torpedoes at a Japanese ship he had disabled. Noting that nine did not explode, he returned to Pearl Harbor with his last torpedo as evidence of the need for further testing. The main "gremlin" turned out to be in the exploder mechanism.

In September 1943 Lockwood's submariners began to receive considerable numbers of far-ranging fleet submarines and torpedoes that worked. American subs took a fairly small toll of Japan's 6.9 million tons of shipping, until December 1943. Between then and the end of hostilities in August 1945, however, they reduced enemy shipping to 1.8

million tons; most of the remaining vessels operated in the Sea of Japan. The rapid demise of the enemy merchant marine during the final twenty months of the war markedly affected Japanese industrial output by depriving it of raw materials. By cutting off the rich oil stores in Southeast Asia, the interdicting submarines, backed by Allied aircraft, caused Japanese pilot training to be curtailed and led the First Mobile Fleet to be based at Tawitawi in the southern Philippines, where the ships had access to Borneo oil but were far from fleet repair facilities in Singapore and Japan.

The American submarines' effectiveness was greatly improved not only because the boats and torpedoes were better designed and more plentiful but also because American underseas tactics were sharpened with combat experience. And the skippers had growing amounts of information on the locations of enemy vessels from Ultra communications intelligence intercepts. Lockwood's submarines played major roles in winning the two largest naval battles of the Pacific conflict—Philippine Sea and Leyte Gulf. Altogether eleven hundred Japanese merchant ships and two hundred combat ships were sunk by American subs, far exceeding the numbers destroyed by Allied aircraft and naval surface ships together. The Pacific Fleet's submarine force lost fifty-four boats during the war.

Unfortunately, the potency of the American submarines and planes in interdicting enemy shipping led to the killing of a large number of American and Allied prisoners of war. As the American advance neared the Philippines in 1944, the Japanese forced POWs in prison camps in that archipelago and elsewhere in Southeast Asia to board ships for transfer to camps in Formosa, Manchuria, Korea, and Japan. The living conditions in the holds of these ships were so terrible that multitudes of already emaciated or diseased captives died en route. Most of the losses came, however, when the "Hell Ships" were struck by American subs or aircraft that had no knowledge of the ships' pathetic passengers. The principal sinkings of prison ships took place between September 1944 and January 1945. Among the worst tragedies, one prison ship was torpedoed off Mindanao in early September, with 670 prisoners killed; in late October another was sunk in the South China Sea, 1,780 prisoners dying; in mid-December a prison ship was bombed in Subic Bay in the Philippines as it prepared to depart, with 900 POWs killed, many of the rest losing their lives when the next ship they boarded was sunk off Formosa.

In addition to their devastating capabilities as offensive weapons, working singly or in groups, Lockwood's submarines made other valuable contributions. They rescued airmen and seamen from downed planes and sunken ships. They supplied coast-watchers at lonely tracking posts in the Solomons and guerrilla bands in the Philippines and other occupied territories. And they gathered intelligence data on enemy ships and shore activities while on cruises.

The first squadrons of Boeing B-29 "Superfortresses," the only very-long-range bombers that saw action in large numbers in World War II, were dispatched to bases near Calcutta, India, in the spring of 1944. Organized as the XX Bomber Command, these planes could strike targets fifteen hundred miles away while carrying bomb loads of ten tons each. They were well armed and sturdily built. The B-29s also flew faster than most fighters and reached extremely high altitudes. The first B-29 raids targeted Thailand and Kyushu in June, flying from new bases built by coolie labor in West China. The lack of overland supply routes into China meant that the B-29s often had to transport their own fuel, bombs, and other supplies from India over the Himalayas to China, which considerably hampered their effectiveness and made General Curtis LeMay, head of the XX Bomber Command, want a better location for the big bombers.

That solution came with the conquest of the Marianas and the building of B-29 bases on Saipan, Tinian, and Guam in the early fall of 1944. B-29 missions from the Marianas, handled by the XXI Bomber Command, were inaugurated in October with a strike against Truk. Less than a month later they began raiding Japan, beginning with a one-hundred-bomber attack on Tokyo. For the next month or so they conducted missions against targets in Japan, employing one hundred or more B-29s on each attack. Besides interceptions by Japanese fighters rising from Iwo Jima, enemy aircraft over Japan provided strong resistance at first, with more than two hundred fighters often hitting the B-29 formations. By the end of December the XXI Command's performances were causing anxiety for Arnold, the de jure head of the Twentieth Air Force (the B-29s), because of losses that were higher than projected, poor weather conditions and visibility at the high altitudes then used for dropping bombs, and disappointing records of bombs on targets. Arnold decided to transfer LeMay to the Marianas in January and to move his old XX Bomber Command of B-29s in India and China to the islands in April. In the spring of 1945 he sent Major General Nathan F. Twining from Europe to the Marianas to take command of the Twentieth Air Force.

LeMay decided in February to alter tactics drastically by terminating high-explosive, high-altitude attacks in favor of incendiary bombing at low levels. The first raid under LeMay's new plan was memorable: an attack on Tokyo during the night of March 9–10, 1945, by more than 330 B-29s carrying nearly 1,700 tons of incendiary bombs. More than 83,000 people were killed, 100,000 were wounded, and fifteen square miles of Tokyo were destroyed. Firestorms of great speed swept some areas of the city and proved to be more destructive of people and property than the atomic bomb attacks on Hiroshima and Nagasaki. Four times in the next ten days B-29 missions hit Japanese cities with similar fire raids, dropping three times the tonnage of bombs that had been used in the previous hundred days. Significant to Arnold and LeMay, only 22 B-29s were downed during almost 1,600 sorties in that ten-day span. The contribution of Iwo Jima in navigational and emergency landing assistance helped, as did the enemy fighters' decreased effectiveness at night.

In early April long-range P-51s, as well as P-47s with supplementary fuel tanks, arrived on Iwo Jima, thereafter providing welcome fighter escorts for the B-29s. Immediately the losses of the big bombers started to decline while the destruction of Japanese fighters mounted. From May until the war's termination in mid-August, American and Allied planes enjoyed control of the skies over Japan. Besides the aircraft based on the Marianas and Iwo Jima, by the late spring planes were hitting the Japanese home islands from the Philippines and from Pacific Fleet carriers, adding a round-the-clock pattern of destructiveness which exceeded that wreaked on Nazi Germany.

In April the last of the B-29s from India and China arrived in the Marianas while more of the bombers reached the islands from the United States. Soon the downtown areas of Japan's largest two dozen cities had been devastated. B-29s as well as other bombers were used to drop mines in all important harbors of Japan's home islands. The miseries of the Japanese populace were growing fast by summer, with food scarce, most factories ruined, electrical and water services disrupted, millions homeless, epidemic diseases spreading, fire equipment worn out or destroyed, and morale nearing collapse. In July, General Spaatz, who had headed the American strategic bombing program in Europe, arrived on Guam to establish the headquarters of his new command, U.S. Strategic Air Forces, Pacific. It provided centralized control over the bombing campaign that now had grown to include many thousands of planes from the Twentieth, Fifth, Thirteenth, and Seventh air forces and the Fast Carrier Force. In addition, the Third Fleet's warships were boldly staging bombardments along the coasts of Japan.

On August 6 a B-29 named the *Enola Gay* lifted off a runway on Tinian and began its flight toward Japan. Its target was Hiroshima, where it opened a new era of horror in warfare by dropping a single atomic bomb. More than 78,000 people died and 70,000 were injured that day, with many thousands more dying later; two-thirds of the city's buildings were destroyed. Before Tokyo authorities could accurately assess what had happened at Hiroshima and consider the implications for Japan's course in the war, a second B-29 from Tinian delivered another atomic bomb, this time on the port of Nagasaki. The destruction was staggering, but less than at Hiroshima, because of the hilly terrain of the city that shielded some areas. Almost 40,000 people died and 25,000 were wounded, again with thousands dying later from injuries and radiation illnesses; about half or less of the city's structures were wiped out.

Besides trying to adjust to the shock of this second atomic strike, Japan's leaders were confronted with another ominous turn of events. The Soviet Union, with whom Tokyo had been secretly, if futilely, negotiating for a conditional peace with the Allies, went to war against Japan on August 8. At Yalta in February 1945, as well as on two earlier occasions, Stalin had promised to enter the war against Japan within three months after Germany's surrender. Soviet forces overran Manchuria and the northern part of Korea before Japan surrendered on the 15th. The two atomic bombs, the Soviet entry into the war in the Far East, and the disintegration of the Japanese economy and morale were the key factors underlying Japan's decision to capitulate.

In November 1944 the Joint Staff Planners of the JCS had started work on plans for the invasion of Japan, though the issue of a ground assault was not settled. The Joint Chiefs of Staff late that month approved their planning drafts for Operation Olympic, an invasion of Kyushu, and Operation Coronet, an amphibious assault on Honshu. The operations on Leyte, Iwo Jima, Okinawa, and Luzon each lasted far longer than anticipated, so it was early April before the JCS directed MacArthur and Nimitz to start planning for Olympic, scheduled to be launched November 1, 1945, with MacArthur as overall ground commander and Nimitz as

naval chief. At the same time the JCS modified the Pacific
command arrangement so that it could align forces for the
thrusts into Japan. MacArthur retained his command over the
Southwest Pacific Area but now assumed the added position
of head of U.S. Army Forces, Pacific. Nimitz's titles were
unchanged since he kept command of the Pacific Ocean
Areas and, as Pacific Fleet commander, already had the
counterpart of MacArthur's new post.

The realignment of forces by services under the two
commanders did not solve precisely the problem of their
parameters of command, and typical interservice squabbling
ensued among planners in Washington and at the two
Pacific headquarters. By June 18, when the Joint Chiefs met
with Truman at the White House, most command matters
had been settled, and the president ordered the JCS to
authorize Olympic. All was not resolved yet, says the main
historian of the invasion planning: "The president added
only one proviso—that he be given another review before
the operation began. Even then, all hoped that somehow the
war could be ended short of invasion." Two days earlier
Truman had received news of another option: the first
atomic bomb had been successfully tested at Alamogordo,
New Mexico.

The redeployment of ground and air units from the
European and Mediterranean theaters and the development
of bases in the Pacific for staging Olympic and Coronet
proved more complicated than expected by MacArthur and
Nimitz. As throughout the war, shipping loomed as a major
troublemaker; there were never enough merchant ships,
troop transports, lighters, port personnel, and landing craft.
Both theaters began large-scale roll-ups of equipment and
supplies, moving to staging bases in the Philippines and
Marianas the bulk of war materiel that was still usable from
facilities now in back areas to the south.

The principal objective of Olympic was to secure naval,
air, and logistical bases to support the critical, larger assault
the next spring on Honshu, the main home island of Japan.

The spearhead of the Kyushu assault was to be made by Krueger's Sixth Army, which would be supported by the Fifth and Seventh fleets and aircraft of the Far East Air Forces, the Twentieth Air Force, and the Fast Carrier Force. Actually, Olympic plans, as well as unit training for the assault, were still in the formative stage when V-J Day (August 15) was proclaimed, marking Japan's capitulation.

The plans for Coronet, the spring invasion of Honshu, were at an early stage when the war suddenly ended. In Coronet, MacArthur again was to command ground and army air operations, while Nimitz would command sea and naval air operations. The Honshu assault would involve Eichelberger's Eighth Army and Hodges's First Army from Europe. In an early draft of the plan, Stilwell's Tenth Army was to be employed in the initial Coronet assault but was not so designated in later plans. If Japanese resistance was formidable and could not be broken reasonably soon in the Honshu assault, MacArthur intended to use a number of Australian, British, New Zealand, French, and Canadian divisions that were included as reserves.

The plan for entering Japan that was finally put into effect after Japan's surrender was MacArthur's Blacklist Plan. It called for a coordinated movement of ground, naval, and air forces into the four Japanese home islands, with the U.S. Eighth Army carrying the main responsibility for the military administration of the occupation. Neither Washington leaders nor MacArthur envisioned a genuinely Allied occupation. The Allies would have token forces in Japan and would offer counsel on policymaking, but the United States would keep a tight grip on the actual planning and implementing of occupation policies and programs. The Soviets protested loudest about the American show MacArthur would run. East-West tensions ran high over postwar Japan in one of the earliest harbingers of the approaching cold war.

Churchill commented after the war, "Of all the amazing deeds of bravery of the war, I regard MacArthur's personal landing at Atsugi as the greatest of the lot." The general arrived on August 30 at Atsugi Airfield, a former kamikaze base near Yokohama, by which time only a marine regiment and an airborne division represented the Allies in Japan. Fanatics opposed to the surrender had been stirring up serious trouble in the Tokyo area for two weeks, and MacArthur could easily have become a target. His bold gamble paid off, however, and he set up his headquarters undisturbed at a Yokohama hotel where he remained until he moved to the U.S. embassy in Tokyo six days after the surrender ceremony.

The formal surrender on September 2, unlike those for Germany, was elaborate. Hundreds of senior officers representing the thirteen Allied nations at war against Japan assembled on the quarterdeck of the battleship *Missouri*, anchored in Tokyo Bay amid over a thousand American and Allied ships, mostly of Halsey's Third Fleet. This array of Allied firepower became even more impressive to correspondents and the Japanese delegation when additional Allied might was exhibited in a dramatic fly-over by four hundred B-29s and fifteen hundred carrier planes.

MacArthur had been appointed supreme commander for the Allied powers to accept the surrender and to head the Allied occupation of Japan. The general presided over the ceremony with dignity and warned in a moving address: "We must go forward to preserve in peace what we have won in war.... We have had our last chance. If we do not now devise some greater and more equitable system, Armageddon will be at our door." All present must have realized that the nature of war had changed with the dawning of the atomic era.

PART FOUR

Overview

16

Tribulations of the GI

THE CHASM BETWEEN senior commanders and enlisted men in the armed forces has normally been wide but never more so than in the Second World War. In the American services this could be attributed to the unprecedented size of the ground, sea, and air forces, the complex organization that underlay the chain of command, and the distance that usually separated theater headquarters from the frontlines.

The life of the fighting man is hard to capsulize in any war, so much do individual circumstances vary, but the overseas conditions of the American enlisted man, or "GI," of World War II are especially difficult to summarize. For one thing, though most of the men were in the army ground forces, there were also record numbers in the navy, marines, and Coast Guard. Even for army soldiers in ground units, their environments and problems varied depending on whether they were in infantry, artillery, armor, or support/service forces. By far, infantrymen were subjected to more combat and thus more casualties than any other branch; their likelihood of succumbing to combat fatigue (shock) was understandably higher too. The living conditions faced by American troops differed greatly according to their global deployment, ranging from the European and Mediterranean theaters of operation to the China-Burma-India theater and the Southwest Pacific and Pacific Ocean Areas theaters.

Despite the widely different ethnic, cultural, and geographic situations in which American troops around the world found themselves, they had a remarkable number of experiences in common. In battle they were confused by the fog of war that seemed to blanket all arenas of deadly collision, whether in ground, sea, or air warfare: the scattering of units, the contrasts between well-laid plans and unexpected realities, the frustration and fear of not knowing where and when danger lurked, and the inability to grasp the broad picture of the course of battle. Sensory experiences are the main links between fighting men on all fronts, as well as with the participants in battles of wars past: the unbelievable noise of exploding shells, the smell of dead humans and horses, the sight of heads and limbs blown from bodies, and the varying feels of the foxhole—mud, dust, snow, and blood.

An astonishing proportion of American servicemen, at any given moment, were caught in what General Lesley McNair, head of army ground forces, called "overhead." They were, he explained, "the invisible horde of people going here and there but seemingly never arriving." On other occasions he referred to this traffic as "pipelines" that were jammed with casuals from replacement and reassignment depots, troops on furlough, and others in transit. In May 1945 the U.S. army comprised 8.3 million troops, of whom 2.1 million were in ground combat units, 2.4 million in air combat units, 1.6 million in service units, and an amazing 2.2 million in "overhead" or "pipelines."

It has been estimated that the army ground forces had twenty-two men for every one who served in action, so long was the logistical train and so large "the invisible horde." No other nation's forces approximated the American in the high standard of living maintained for men overseas, a fact that explains both the friction with other Allied personnel and the U.S. ground forces' lack of ground mobility in the absence of ports, roads, and rail lines.

The confusion of the worldwide movement of large numbers of Americans in uniform, though perhaps inevitable, led to the "hurry up and wait" pattern that all enlisted men, who understood the reasons less than their officers, came to despise. In all services the average individual probably spent more hours of sheer boredom and inactivity than he did in performing official duties.

In common with troops of all wars, most men in the ranks in 1941–1945 also shared two other experiences. First, they developed real or imagined grievances against officers, usually at the small-unit level, for few knew officers at higher levels. Though striking or even killing officers was not rare, mutinies were uncommon until the wars in Europe and the Pacific ended and some small units staged violent demonstrations to protest their retention overseas longer than they thought necessary. Most enlisted men vented their hatred of officers by abundant griping, making signs ridiculing the detested superior, or faking their performance of chores he had ordered.

On all fronts in the Second World War, as in the Great War of 1914–1918, American and other enlisted men also shared the never-ending job of "digging in" and protecting themselves in holes and sometimes trenches, both on the frontline and at bases within range of enemy bombing, strafing, or naval shelling. Entrenching tools and shovels became as vital to the infantrymen (70 percent of ground combat forces) as their rifles. The care with which they prepared their positions in the ground, whether soft soil, hard clay, rock, or sand, often determined their fate. Authorities have estimated that artillery shells killed or wounded more Americans in World War II than any other weapon. Digging in was better protection against rifle or machine-gun bullets, but it also saved many men during artillery barrages.

Terrain and climate conditions could make life miserable at the front or behind the lines in any of the theaters of operations. Many Americans assigned to Northwest Africa or Italy arrived in the theater expecting to find "the sunny Mediterranean" of travel advertisements. The war in Algeria and Tunisia saw disappointing early progress for Allied forces partly because of torrential rains. "In terms of false expectations," says a noted historian, "Italy was undoubtedly the most unpleasant surprise to troops who served there." The American Fifth Army, as well as the British forces on its eastern flank, endured rains and floods in the autumn and spring of both their years of campaigning on the peninsula. They also had to live and fight through the two worst winters Italy had known in two decades. Most of the Americans on the front underwent miserable ordeals in the snow and ice that plagued them in the Apennine Mountains, which ran almost the length of the peninsula and where much of the heaviest fighting occurred. Cases of frostbite, pneumonia, influenza, and other ailments associated with living outside in foxholes and trenches during heavy rains or snows were common.

In the offensives across France and Germany, Americans suffered through miserable periods of torrential rains, heavy floods, and deep snows and ice. American soldiers engaged in the long, bloody campaign of the Hürtgen Forest, south of Aachen, Germany, faced terrible conditions in the drenching downpours and freezing winter conditions in the rugged terrain. Likewise, troops involved in the Battle of the Bulge were hit by both a surprise German offensive and, said one American participant, "the meanest winter in thirty-eight years" in the Ardennes region. During the battle for Bastogne the temperature was often "a steady zero." Even after the Germans were repulsed, one U.S. division in the area "was losing 100 men a day from illnesses attributable to the snow and cold." Of course, such extreme weather conditions were not continually present, but the worst rain and snow in decades meant ordeals for the GIs in digging or living in foxholes, some of which had to be blown out of frozen ground with explosives.

Terrain and climate problems for Americans in the war against Japan were different but also more damaging to the GIs' general combat effectiveness. The distances involved in the Pacific were nightmarish enough for logistical planners in terms of sheer mileage, but the character of that mileage was even more staggering, comprising some of the most impenetrable combinations of jungles, marshes, and mountains in the world, especially in the Southwest and South Pacific theaters and in Burma. Few terrain studies were available, for many of the islands and their coastal waters were uncharted before the war. Harbors were few in number and poor in quality, as were potential sites for airfields.

The intense heat, high humidity, and frequent torrential rains, along with the hostile terrain, plagued men and equipment. Health conditions were especially poor in Burma and on New Guinea, the Solomons, New Britain, and the Admiralties. Awaiting Allied and Japanese personnel without discrimination were a host of hideous tropical diseases that could sicken or kill troops almost as fast as a bullet: malaria, dengue fever, tropical ulcers, blackwater fever, bacillary and amoebic dysentery, scrub typhus, ringworm, hookworm, yaws, cholera, and yellow fever, to name some. Clouds of mosquitoes, flies, leeches, chiggers, and other disease-carrying creepy, crawly creatures made epidemic disease an unrelenting foe for fighting men on both sides. Losses to disease, as well as to serious related morale problems, were far higher in combat zones near the equator in the Pacific than in the Mediterranean or European theaters.

In spite of the tribulations of enemy fire, adverse terrain and climate, and strange diseases, American fighting men who were injured or wounded in World War II had a better chance of surviving than their counterparts in any earlier conflict, thanks to the marvels of American medical progress and its adaptation to military needs. Probably no other period in medical history produced so many innovations. Penicillin and other new antibiotics revolutionized the treatment of numerous life-threatening conditions suffered by the troops. Plasma and whole-blood transfusions saved many injured boys. New medicines were introduced to combat epidemics and cure tropical afflictions.

Military medical organization was restructured to make

possible surgical attention for wounded troops near the battlefront, with quick air transportation to more advanced facilities in the rear. Psychiatrists and psychologists treated and counseled men suffering from combat fatigue, returning many of them to their units. Corpsmen may have outdone every other type of battlefield participant in demonstrating bravery under fire when bringing wounded men back into American lines. Nurses served closer to the front than ever before and demonstrated professionalism and courage under fire. The Army Nurse Corps boasted 59,000 nurses, the most of any of the armed services. The new medical practices and inventions made World War II "the first American war in which more men died in combat than of disease." According to an authority on military medicine in the war, "Despite the proliferation of lethal new weaponry, American battle death rates shrank by about half, disease death rates by twenty-seven times [compared with World War I.]"

Americans overseas had to adjust to ethnic and cultural circumstances in the nations in which they were stationed. In nations like India or China where religions, cultures, and mores were different, the incoming Yankees not infrequently ran afoul of local customs and values when they ventured from their bases into local towns and cities. Sometimes there were clashes, but more often than not the natives were so grateful to have the Americans, whether for their protection or their affluence, that they tolerated their blunders. The natives generally knew more about American ways than the troops knew about theirs.

Frequently the worst collisions, along with the most fraternization and marriages with locals, took place in Britain, Australia, and New Zealand and, to a lesser extent, in France and Italy. In these more industrialized countries, the residents looked on GIs as a necessary nuisance for the duration of the war, ostracizing them from higher social circles. Servicemen of those nations resented the higher pay scales of the Yanks as well as their boisterous behavior on furlough weekends and particularly their relations with the local troops' girlfriends and wives. Whatever the dislikes of locals for Americans, and vice versa, a considerable number of Americans married women from the United Kingdom and the Commonwealth countries and brought them back to the United States after the war.

With the French and Italians, the American troops' record of harmonious relations was somewhat spotty. At the time of the Normandy invasion in 1944, for instance, for every French village that welcomed them with open arms, the citizens of another resented them for making their region a battlefield. Italian townsfolk, likewise, seemed to receive Americans either warmly or indifferently based upon the amount of destruction the new troops' presence caused, instead of on any remaining allegiance to Mussolini's fascism. As a rule, wherever Americans went they had three things in their favor in winning over the locals: their money, their abundance of food gifts, and their unpretentious friendliness.

The most serious trouble—indeed, considerable violence— occurred in Australia, where the Aussies widely endorsed the concept of keeping their continent as purely white as possible. They deeply resented the U.S. army's stationing many of its African American soldiers "Down Under." After several racist-motivated riots and murders, and complaints from Australian officers, MacArthur finally transferred most of the African Americans to New Guinea and northward where they served principally in service units. Guam too experienced an ugly race riot, but the fight was between black and white sailors and marines. As customary in the American armed forces, of course, there were periodic brawls between men of the different services; the usual matchings were army against navy, or navy versus marine.

The prejudice of white American servicemen was so deeply entrenched in the early 1940s that African American units and individuals were not allowed to mesh harmoniously in the American forces. One authority says that black leaders believed, "with good reason," that African American troops were largely relegated to low-level labor duties because of "white stereotyping" of them as "timid, untrainable, and useful only for manual labor."

The two largest black units that served in combat were the Ninety-third Infantry Division, which saw action on Bougainville, Morotai, and Saipan, and the Ninety-second Infantry Division, which engaged in combat in North Italy. Perhaps the finest combat records of African Americans were those of the Ninety-ninth Pursuit Squadron, the first air unit comprised solely of African Americans, and the 332nd Fighter Group, which contained six hundred airmen trained at Tuskegee Institute, Alabama, and flew more than two hundred missions escorting American bombers over Europe. The African American pilots destroyed 111 enemy aircraft in the air and 150 others on the ground, and in their escorting did not lose a single bomber to enemy fighters. The Ledo Road in Burma was built by Chinese and American soldiers and civilian laborers, with African American troops constituting 60 percent of the fifteen thousand American Yanks involved.

In all, more than a million African American men and women served in the U.S. armed forces in the Second World War, most of them in the army and the Women's Army Corps. More than 500,000 of them served overseas, but, sadly, a reliable source reports that "they were often better treated by the Europeans and Asians, including defeated enemy civilians, than they were by their white fellow GIs."

In the spring of 1942 Congress passed measures providing for the establishment of women's "auxiliary" forces, which entitled them to serve but afforded lower pay and benefits than for male GIs. This inequity was partially corrected in late 1943 by further legislation that gave the female volunteers full status ostensibly in their service, as well as equal pay and equivalent ranks. More than eighty thousand women served in the navy, marines, and Coast Guard, while nearly double that number joined the Women's Army Corps.

The idea of women in uniform was as difficult for white

male GIs to accept as was the amalgamation of African Americans into the services, especially overseas. Uniformed women sent overseas generally performed at extremely high levels and tolerated far more bias and abuse than they had suffered at home. There was no question, however, that the more than 230,000 women in uniform released at least that number or more male servicemen to serve in combat, support, and service functions at or near the fronts. The war "indelibly altered the role of women in American society" because of their achievements in both industry and the armed services. Later official reports, if not widespread public recognition, pointed to "the highly skilled jobs which the majority of WACS [and other American women in uniform] eventually held, because such positions often carried with them significant responsibility." Actually, "many people doubted that women were capable of handling such jobs" until they proved their worth in the Second World War.

Hitler based his Nazi ideological crusade, in part, on the ethnic and racial supremacy of the Aryans who in Germany were to become "the super race." This culminated in his ruthless purging of more than twelve million Jews and other "undesirables." His armed forces, however, seldom exhibited such attitudes toward captured or cornered Anglo-American troops, though they treated trapped or imprisoned Soviet soldiers unmercifully. In turn, Americans in the war against Germany became fully persuaded of the evil nature of Nazism and its political leaders, but most of them respected German fighting men as worthy adversaries and their senior commanders as responsible professionals.

The ninety thousand Americans held as prisoners of war by Germany were treated considerably better in most camps than the fifteen thousand to twenty thousand Americans imprisoned by the Japanese. Sixty percent of the latter prisoners died before hostilities ceased.

An official study states that American troops were accustomed to 3,300 calories a day while Japanese soldiers were used to 1,500 calories. If the American prisoners had been given the ration the Japanese received—which seldom happened but was called for by the Geneva Prisoner of War Convention of 1929—they would slowly have starved in view of the heavy manual work the enemy guards forced them to do. More than this, the Yanks and other Allied POWs were usually deprived of Red Cross supplements in Japanese-run prisons, while Americans in German camps got the German troops' base rations of 2,500 calories daily plus all the Red Cross parcels that arrived. At Stalag Luft III, near Sagan, Germany, the weekly box usually contained powdered milk, Spam, corned beef, liver paste, salmon, margarine, biscuits, coffee, jam or preserves, prunes or raisins, sugar, chocolate bars, soap bars, and cigarettes, according to a prison record. On the other hand, Japanese guards frequently confiscated incoming Red Cross supplies for their own use, often consuming them in full view of the emaciated POWs.

Hard labor, frequent penalties, and severe physical punishment were far more common in Japanese than German POW camps. The harsher treatment can be explained partially by the Japanese belief that the prisoners did not deserve more daily calories than their own troops were receiving and by the traditional Japanese view that surrender was a humiliating act to which only weak, dishonorable soldiers yielded.

The treatment received by American prisoners from the Germans was favorable only in contrast to prison experiences under the Japanese. Living, or simply surviving, in any Axis prison camp was a tribulation for all American and Allied personnel. It was an ordeal wherein harshness ranged from severe to moderate; it was rarely light for any prisoner physically, emotionally, or psychologically. Most American POWs found the postwar consequences were ruined health and careers. They were largely forgotten by the American people and media. A few nations' official histories of World War II include a volume on their men who were captured, but the American military establishment's official chronicles ignore the history of its prisoners of war. Like the scores of millions of civilians caught in lines of fire between battling forces, the story of the POWs remains largely untold.

17

The War in Retrospect

WORLD WAR II cast long shadows on the development of American society and the nation's economy. The revolutions in political, economic, and social rights for women, African Americans, Latinos, and Native Americans originated with the opportunities they found during the conflict to demonstrate their worth in war industries and the armed services. Indeed, it was the beginning of a long, complex, and often tortuous series of efforts by the federal government to use the armed forces, especially the army, as a giant experiment in the integration of women and minorities.

The war years also marked the clear emergence of the military-industrial complex that has characterized much of the largest corporations' efforts and influences on the Pentagon, which became the country's largest consumer by far. This growing complex came to encompass scientists and engineers at leading research universities through the cornucopia of unbelievably large federal and corporate grants.

In addition, the American people came to see the war years as a golden era of national unity when the citizenry overwhelmingly united to fight "the good war" against the evils of totalitarianism. This romanticized view gained credence as Americans looked back on the Second World War in the disturbing aftermaths of the inconclusive Korean War and the bitter setback of the Vietnam conflict. A widespread nostalgia was born that has made the music of the age, books about the war, and celebratory commemorations increasingly in vogue. The dark sides of the war period in the forty-eight states and overseas have been largely suppressed in this understandable but not entirely rational phenomenon.

For the American armed forces, World War II left important long-range results. Even though the nation's largest wars after 1945 were in Korea and Vietnam, the leadership of the military establishment and thus the setting of strategic priorities and allocations for the services remained for the most part firmly in the hands of European-theater veterans, at least until the 1960s. This was particularly true of the uniformed heads of the army, by far the largest service, whose first chief of staff from the Pacific war was General George H. Decker in 1960–1962. Air force chiefs of staff, except one, were from the European air war until 1965, and all but two of the JCS chairmen were Europe-oriented until 1964. In pushing his proposals for the occupation of Japan and the Korean conflict, MacArthur, an ardent Pacific-first advocate, was painfully aware of the European bent in the State Department as well as in the Pentagon and the White House. In view of this trend, which paralleled the focus of the postwar media, especially after the Marshall Plan and the creation of NATO (North Atlantic Treaty Organization), perhaps it was to be expected that the only two-term president of the first decades after World War II was Dwight Eisenhower.

The sometimes bitter interservice rivalries, especially in the Pacific, that erupted during the years 1941–1945 led to wartime planning to resolve this ugly situation after the war. It enjoyed mixed success in the landmark National Security Acts of 1947 and 1949.* Other consequences for the services

*The earlier measure set up the National Military Establishment, consisting of the Office of the Secretary of Defense; the departments of the Army (formerly War), Navy, and Air Force; the National Security Council; and the Central Intelligence Agency. The act two years later established the Department of Defense and strengthened the power of the secretary of defense and the chairman of the Joint Chiefs of Staff. It also removed the three service department secretaries from cabinet-level status. All these administrative changes were intended to improve interservice relations.

were untold future benefits from the revolution in military technology and medicine that began during the Second World War. Britain was a rival in many of these areas in the war, but in the postwar decades the United States became the clear leader in military medicine and gained superiority over the Soviet Union in most frontiers of weaponry.

U.S. military services benefited from the new thinking of 1941–1945, especially stimulated by the British, on the futility of sound military strategy when subject to inconsistent national strategy, and on the necessity in coalition warfare of compromise, interdependence, and coordination. The Americans also learned new respect for the significance of logistics as perhaps the most vital factor in determining the outcome of campaigns, and they began senior service-school studies on the inseparability of strategy and logistics. Also, because of the confusion in strategy that ensued in the aftermath of the use of nuclear warfare, and the need for a continuing alliance with the onset of the cold war, the Anglo-American military partnership continued after 1945 to share technology, intelligence, and strategic plans. Britons had been Uncle Sam's indispensable, if increasingly unequal, friends during wartime, and the "special relationship" continued despite the decline of Britain's political, military, and economic clout.

The war now seems to have been a turning point in the nature of nationalism. It signaled both the end of rampant large-scale ultranationalism as practiced by advanced but aggressive powers like Germany, Italy, and Japan, and the outbreak of unpredictable, backward small-state nationalist movements and their "people's wars." Such conflicts were precipitated often by communism but also incorporated novel forms of nationalism. The new developments led American strategic planners to prepare for military contingencies that could not be resolved by attempting to refight the war of 1941–1945 or by employing massive nuclear retaliation.

American contributions in overwhelming firepower and massive material assistance were crucial to defeating perhaps the finest ground force in history, the German army, and in forcing the capitulation of all three members of the Axis. The prowess of the German war machine has been so highly praised that it needs to be emphasized that in the long run the Allies virtually annihilated it, with the Americans and their abundant weapons playing a large part. Of course, the Pacific phase of the war with Japan was almost entirely an American show. Unlike World War I, America's military role in the later world conflict was unquestionably decisive, not only in American leaders' strategic and logistical planning but also in the implementing of operations on both sides of the globe.

Even the British sometimes suspected that the Americans preferred to achieve victory by substituting overwhelming firepower for combat personnel. In war costs it is true that the U.S. contribution in World War II was anomalous. Financially, the conflict was more expensive for the United States than for any other belligerent, in large measure because of its role as "the arsenal of democracy" for all the Allies. In terms of military and civilian deaths, however, the United States suffered fewer than 300,000, a small proportion of the worldwide total of 55 million to 80 million dead. In hindsight, some authorities have claimed that America's major contribution in materiel rather than in personnel was deliberately planned so that the Soviet Union and Germany would bear the heaviest human losses. There is no evidence for this, however, and, besides, it attributes more ingenuity in American wartime planning than existed. Moreover, American casualties were among the costliest in the huge European and Pacific campaigns from the summer of 1944 to the war's end.

Much has been written about the racism and ethnocentrism of the European war, especially with regard to Nazi Germany. The hatefulness bred by German propaganda, however, did not carry over into the attitudes and behavior of most of their troops on the Western Front, with the notable exception of the Malmédy massacre during the

Battle of the Bulge. Many American troops had a favorable attitude toward their German opponents on the battlefield, and most of the American public consistently displayed more animosity toward Japan than Germany throughout the war. Some critics of the use of the atomic bombs on Japan have argued, with little plausibility, that Japan, rather than Germany, was targeted because the Japanese were yellow and the Germans were white, and because the United States had a large German American population. This charge of racism fails to explain how the Manhattan Project could have been accelerated in time to produce atomic bombs for attacks on Germany before early May 1945.

On the other hand, new research reveals that race hatred played a far larger role in the Pacific-Asia conflict than in the European-Mediterranean war. Racial stereotypes and hate-mongering by both sides, especially between Japanese and Americans, resulted in propaganda and behavior that were more merciless, dehumanizing, and savage than normally seen in the war with Germany and Italy. American troops represented the leader of the Western world, while Japanese fighting men came from an equally proud nation that had outdistanced all other Asian countries in military and industrial power. Thus Japan saw itself as the champion of the yellow race and America of the white race. The whites had been badly beaten at the start of the war and humiliatingly run out of their imperial domains in Asia and the Pacific, boasted the Japanese.

While the Japanese saw Americans as overrated, lacking in character, uncultured, calloused, ignorant of other societies, and poor in fighting prowess, the American troops, through prewar and wartime indoctrination in countless ways, were conditioned to picture the Japanese as "apes, lesser men, primitives, children, madmen." They became convinced that "the Japanese were a uniquely contemptible and formidable foe who deserved no mercy and virtually demanded extinction," according to an eminent authority. It was ironic that when the war ended the Americans were able to administer the occupation, with strong Japanese assistance, for more than six years in such a way that the two nations emerged from it friends and cold war allies.

For the United States, the Second World War demanded an unprecedented expenditure of funds and energies to build what Roosevelt called "the arsenal of democracy." At a cost of $350 billion, its material contributions to its own armed forces and to the other twenty-five Allied nations were instrumental to operational successes in all theaters around the world. Its peak strength of armed forces was 12.4 million in 1945, surpassed only by the Soviet Union's 12.5 million among all Allied and Axis military totals. American casualties were huge compared with figures for previous wars of the United States, except the Civil War, where nearly all on both sides were Americans. U.S. military deaths in action were 235,000, with 671,000 wounded and 115,000 taken prisoner.

Yet no American homes or buildings were destroyed by enemy fire, except a few by offshore submarines, and no enemy forces invaded any part of the forty-eight states. The nation in 1944–1945 seemed to have achieved total mobilization of its manpower and economic resources, but later studies indicated that the manpower limit had been reached in 1944 at the same time that industry was beginning to curtail war contracts. The production goals needed to finish the war had been topped without pushing outputs to the maximum of economic mobilization.

The American nation performed remarkably at home and on the battlefields, but it is time the romanticism of the good war is laid to rest. For much of the world it was a war of unbridled hate and horror such as men had never known. The Soviet Union and China paid the highest price in property destruction with lengthy frontlines extending across both countries most of the war; more than 25 million Soviet military and civilian dead exceeded the total for any other country, the Chinese ranking second with 15 million military troops and civilians killed.

The statistics of the Second World War for all countries involved are staggering and sobering: military dead and missing, 15 to 20 million; civilian dead and missing, 40 to 60 million; military wounded, 25 million; civilian wounded, 10 to 20 million; homeless, 28 million; prisoners of war, 15 million; civilian prisoners (internees), 20 million; orphans, 5 million; civilians exterminated in concentration camps, 11 to 13 million; economic and financial costs, $1,600 billion. Awesome as these figures are, no human mind can truly conceive the scope and meaning of such losses. Far from being the best and most glorious of wars, it was the worst and most horrible.

A Note on Sources

THE LITERATURE AND unpublished sources on World War II are enormous, and the numbers of books and articles multiply each decade. There are more than twelve thousand books in English on the subject, and many thousands in other languages. The National Archives' holdings of records on the U.S. army in the war weigh over fourteen thousand tons, and these are only a tiny percentage of the original total. The official records of the navy, marines, and other federal agencies related to the wartime military effort also are sizable.

The starting place for the serious student of America's military role in the war are the U.S. official histories: U.S. Army Center of Military History, *United States Army in World War II*, 77 vols. (Washington, D.C., 1949–1993); U.S. Marine Corps Historical Division, *History of U.S. Marine Corps Operations in World War II*, 4 vols. (Washington, D.C., 1958–1968); Samuel E. Morison, *History of United States Naval Operations in World War II*, 15 vols. (Boston, 1947–1962); and Wesley F. Craven and James L. Cate, eds., *The Army Air Forces in World War II*, 7 vols. (Chicago, 1948–1958). All of the U.S. armed services' historical offices have also published series of monographs on specific battles and special topics. A few of the most readable official volumes are cited below.

The main general histories of the Second World War in English have been written by the British, and all slight American contributions to victory. In fact, the most popular history of the war even among American readers today is Winston S. Churchill, *The Second World War*, 6 vols. (London, 1948–1954), which is unabashedly pro-British. The latest and best history by an American is Gerhard L. Weinberg's *World at Arms: A Global History of World War II* (New York, 1994), an excellent study but neglectful of the war with Japan. A potpourri of significant works that cover major topics beyond the bounds of specific theaters are Kent R. Greenfield, ed., *Command Decisions* (New York, 1959), an army volume of collective essays on key strategic decisions affecting ground operations; Paul Fussell, *Wartime: Understanding and Behavior in the Second World War* (New York, 1989), a perceptive examination of psychological and emotional factors affecting the wartime attitudes of common folk and soldiers; John Ellis, *The Sharp End: The Fighting Man in World War II* (New York, 1980), the best coverage of the life of the GI; Gabriel Kolko, *The Politics of War: The World and United States Foreign Policy, 1943–1945* (New York, 1968), a brilliant, provocative attack on conventional views of Allied diplomatic and military policies; John Ellis, *Brute Force: Allied Strategy and Tactics in the Second World War* (New York, 1990), a frank critique of Allied, especially U.S., misuse of industrial superiority and shortsighted tactics against the Axis; Kent R. Greenfield, *American Strategy in World War II: A Reconsideration* (Baltimore, 1963), a good orthodox summary; Samuel E. Morison, *The Two-Ocean Navy: A Short History of the United States Navy in the Second World War* (Boston, 1963), a vividly written account based on his official multivolume history; and Albert C. Cowdrey, *Fighting for Life: American Military Medicine in World War II* (New York, 1994), a much-needed, highly readable, and significant study by an Army historian.

On the American high command, outstanding in fascinating insights and polished style is Robert E. Sherwood, *Roosevelt and Hopkins: An Intimate History* (New York, 1948), revealing early glimpses of key high-level records. Another classic study based on insider access to documents is Herbert Feis, *Churchill, Roosevelt, Stalin: The War They Waged and the Peace They Sought* (Princeton, N.J., 1957). Two army volumes are especially impressive in the coverage of their topics: Maurice Matloff, *Strategic Planning for Coalition Warfare, 1943–1944* (Washington, D.C., 1959), and Robert W. Coakley and Richard W. Leighton, *Global Logistics and Strategy, 1943–1945* (Washington,

D.C., 1968). The only collective studies of the American top commanders are Eric Larrabee, *Commander in Chief: Franklin Delano Roosevelt, His Lieutenants, and Their War* (New York, 1987), which focuses on their relations with Roosevelt; and D. Clayton James and Anne Sharp Wells, *A Time for Giants: Politics of the American High Command in World War II* (New York, 1987), an introduction to the factors underlying the selections for the main commands. The best places to examine the wartime commanders-in-chief, besides Larrabee, are James MacGregor Burns, *Roosevelt: Soldier of Freedom, 1940–1945* (New York, 1970), which stands out among the legions of FDR works, and Harry S. Truman, *Memoirs,* vol. 1, *Year of Decisions, 1945* (Garden City, N.Y., 1955), a blunt and detailed look at the final phase of the war and its aftermath from the White House viewpoint. A much-needed reference work that makes for fascinating reading is Warren Kimball, ed., *Churchill and Roosevelt: The Complete Correspondence,* 3 vols. (Princeton, N.J., 1984). Three of the Joint Chiefs of Staff wrote memoirs, each informative in its own way on the direction of the war: Ernest J. King and Walter M. Whitehill, *Fleet Admiral King: A Naval Record* (New York, 1952), best on Pacific strategy; Henry H. Arnold, *Global Mission* (New York, 1949), strongest on the global problems of running history's largest air force; and William Leahy, *I Was There: The Personal Story of the Chief of Staff to Presidents Roosevelt and Truman* (New York, 1950), by the JCS chairman who served from 1942 to 1949. Outstanding among the biographies of the Joint Chiefs is Forrest C. Pogue, *George C. Marshall,* 4 vols. (New York, 1964–1985), a magisterial monument to a giant among Anglo-American military leaders.

The bibliography of spying and intelligence activities is large, with communications intelligence the most promising frontier for research on World War II. Ronald Lewin is a leader in this field, his publications including two highly acclaimed and intensely interesting studies: *Ultra Goes to War: The First Account of World War II's Greatest Secret Based on Official Documents* (New York, 1978); and *The American Magic:*

Codes, Ciphers, and the Defeat of Japan (New York, 1982). David Kahn is another widely esteemed authority in this area, perhaps his foremost work being *The Codebreakers: The Story of Secret Writing* (New York, 1967), already accepted as a classic on the subject. One of the newest entries is Edward J. Drea, *MacArthur's Ultra: Codebreaking and the War Against Japan* (Lawrence, Kans., 1992), an intriguing glimpse into the baffling world of the Southwest Pacific chief and his unusual intelligence staff and how they used or abused communications intelligence data. The literature on the Office of Strategic Services is rich with exciting memoirs of agents, but the best one-volume history of the organization is R. Harris Smith, *OSS: The Secret History of America's First Central Intelligence Agency* (Berkeley, Calif., 1972).

The complete American ground operations in the European and Mediterranean theaters are covered by only one work, which, though well done, is outdated and excludes the impact of Ultra: Charles B. MacDonald, *The Mighty Endeavor: American Armed Forces in the European Theater in World War II* (New York, 1969). Still the best-written book on both the military and nonmilitary aspects of the war with Germany and Italy is Gordon K. Wright, *The Ordeal of Total War, 1939–1945* (New York, 1968), though it does not give much attention to U.S. forces. Excellent books on other broad topics of the European-Mediterranean conflict are Michael Howard, *The Mediterranean Strategy in the Second World War* (London, 1968), a penetrating analysis by the dean of British military historians; Forrest C. Pogue, *The Supreme Command* (Washington, D.C., 1962), an outstanding official chronicle of Eisenhower's headquarters structure, 1944–1945; and Martin van Creveld, *Fighting Power: Germany and the U.S. Army Performance, 1939–1945* (Westport, Conn., 1982), which, like all his writings, is filled with fresh, provocative insights.

For the two most authoritative recent studies of Operation Overlord, consult Stephen E. Ambrose, *D-Day, June 6, 1944: The Climactic Battle of World War II* (New York, 1994), which highlights the exploits and tragedies of American and Allied troops; and Carlo D'Este, *Decision in Normandy* (New York, 1983), a critical reexamination of the conduct of the American, British, and German operations. A sobering, in-depth study of the performance of American commanders and forces in Northwest Europe is Russell F. Weigley, *Eisenhower's Lieutenants: The Campaign of France and Germany, 1944–1945* (Bloomington, Ind., 1981). Other noteworthy books on the European operations are Charles B. MacDonald, *Company Commander* (Washington, D.C., 1947), the finest memoir by a small-unit commander; Martin Blumenson, *Duel for France, 1944* (Boston, 1963), a vivid account of the advance across France; Cornelius Ryan, *A Bridge Too Far* (New York, 1974), the tragic but action-packed story of Operation Market-Garden; and Charles B. MacDonald, *A Time for Trumpets: The Untold Story of the Battle of the Bulge* (New York, 1985), the foremost of many books on the Ardennes campaign. On American operations in the Mediterranean, the recommended works begin with two by Carlo D'Este: *Bitter Victory: The Battle for Sicily, 1943* (New York, 1988), now the best book on that incomplete victory; and *Fatal Decision: Anzio and the Battle for Rome* (New York, 1991), the most recent and objective analysis of the costly envelopment attempt. On Operation Dragoon, the recent official army volume becomes the standard work: Jeffrey J. Clarke and Robert R. Smith, *Riviera to the Rhine* (Washington, D.C., 1993), which is clear, thorough, and interesting.

American air and naval operations in the Atlantic are best covered in Terry Hughes and John Costello, *The Battle of the Atlantic* (New York, 1977); and Samuel E. Morison, *The Battle of the Atlantic, September 1939–May 1941* (Boston, 1950). As both books properly emphasize, British air and naval forces held center stage for most of that struggle.

The principal works by or about the chief American commanders in the war against Germany and Italy are Stephen E. Ambrose, *The Supreme Commander* (Garden City, N.Y., 1970), both vividly told and authoritative; Martin Blumenson, *The Patton Papers*, 2 vols. (Boston, 1972–1974), a mixture of primary material and biography that provides the most complete look at the fiery general; J. Lawton Collins, *Lightning Joe: An Autobiography* (Baton Rouge, La., 1979), the reminiscences of one of the best American corps commanders; Dwight D. Eisenhower, *Crusade in Europe* (Garden City, N.Y., 1948), largely uncritical but an old best-seller so popular it is still kept in print; and the most recent work, another mixture of reminiscences and biography, Omar N. Bradley and Clay Blair, *A General's Life: An Autobiography* (New York, 1983), which portrays a much more critical Bradley than his 1951 memoir.

The Pacific war has been viewed as "the American conflict" because of the domination of planning and operations by the United States. Two works stand out on the American role against Japan, 1941–1945: Grace P. Hayes, *History of the Joint Chiefs of Staff in World War II: The War Against Japan* (Annapolis, 1982), the only one of three JCS manuscripts on the war to be published; and the much-acclaimed study, Ronald Spector, *Eagle Against the Sun: The American War with Japan* (New York, 1985), which is excellent but sometimes too judgmental on MacArthur. Other recommended general studies of Americans in the war against Japan are Louis Morton, *Strategy and Command: The First Two Years* (Washington, D.C., 1962), a clear delineation of a complex situation and one of the finest of the army series; Jeter A. Isely and Philip A. Crowl, *The U.S. Marines in Amphibious Warfare* (Princeton, N.J., 1951), a thoughtful unofficial analysis of the Central Pacific campaigns by two esteemed official historians; and John Toland, *The Rising Sun: The Decline and Fall of the Japanese Empire* (New York, 1970), a sensitive, empathetic account of the war from the perspective of the Japanese troops.

Books on American battles and campaigns in the Pacific that deserve mention are Louis Morton, *Fall of the Philippines* (Washington, D.C., 1953), the first of his splendid army volumes; John W. Whitman, *Bataan: Our Last Ditch* (New York, 1990), a recent first-rate reexamination of the tragic campaign; Robert Sherrod, *Tarawa: The Story of a Battle* (New York, 1954), a classic by a veteran correspondent with the marines in combat on many islands; Robert Heinl, *Defense at Wake* (Washington, D.C., 1952), one of the best books in the Marine Corps' monograph series; Philip A. Crowl, *Campaign in the Marianas* (Washington, D.C., 1960), a well-done volume in the army series; Richard B. Frank, *Guadalcanal* (New York, 1990), an exhaustive recent history of the campaign that covers all the services well for the first time; C. Vann Woodward, *The Battle for Leyte Gulf* (New York, 1947), old but still outstanding by the later distinguished historian of the New South; Robert R. Smith, *Triumph in the Philippines* (Washington, D.C., 1963), an army volume that lucidly and fairly depicts the Pacific's largest campaign, Luzon; and Samuel E. Morison, *New Guinea and the Marianas, March 1944–August 1944* (Boston, 1964), which covers the Philippine Sea battle and other naval actions with a sailor's eye and a graceful style.

The bibliography on the Pearl Harbor attack is virtually a subfield, so huge has it become. Two books stand out from the rest: Gordon Prange, *At Dawn We Slept* (New York, 1981), objective, careful, and remarkably thorough; and Roberta Wohlstetter, *Pearl Harbor: Warning and Decision* (Stanford, Calif., 1962), a pioneer study emphasizing the complexity of separating "sounds" from "noises" in the radio intercepts and other sources of the pre-assault period.

Two memoirs by Pacific war commanders are especially interesting: William F. Halsey and Joseph Byran, *Admiral Halsey's Story* (New York, 1947), which catches the color, impetuosity, and brilliance of the controversial South Pacific and Third Fleet leader; and Robert L. Eichelberger, *Dear Miss Em: General Eichelberger's War in the Pacific, 1942–45,* ed. Jay Luvaas (Westport, Conn., 1972), a fascinating and humorous look at machinations and characters in the Southwest Pacific high command. At last there is a good study of MacArthur's top lieutenants, in William M. Leary, ed., *We Shall Return! MacArthur's Commanders and the Defeat of Japan* (Lexington, Ky., 1988), which has nine essays by respected scholars. The best of the biographies on Pacific leaders are E. B. Potter, *Nimitz* (Annapolis, 1976), by a respected naval historian and longtime friend of the admiral; Thomas E. Buell, *The Quiet*

Warrior: A Biography of Admiral Raymond Spruance (Boston, 1974), a fine work that places Spruance among the first rank of naval commanders; and D. Clayton James, *The Years of MacArthur,* 3 vols. (Boston, 1970–1985), the first comprehensive study, the second volume covering 1941–1945.

The literature on the war with Japan boasts five works that are especially distinguished as original, worthwhile interpretative endeavors: Christopher Thorne, *Allies of a Kind: The United States, Britain, and the War Against Japan* (London, 1978), a massive, thoughtful treatise not very favorable to Americans; Akira Iriye, *Power and Culture* (Cambridge, Mass., 1981), an unusual reinterpretation of Japanese-American relations, their cultural context, and the two nations' quests for international order; John Dower, *War Without Mercy: Race and Power in the Pacific War* (New York, 1986), a perceptive, if often disturbing, inquiry into the Pacific conflict as rooted in racial hatred and ethnic superiority on both sides; Martin J. Sherwin, *A World Destroyed: The Atomic Bomb and the Grand Alliance* (New York, 1975), which focuses on the impact of the atomic bomb on immediate postwar relations between America, Britain, and the Soviet Union; and Robert J. C. Butow, *Japan's Decision to Surrender* (Stanford, Calif., 1954), a brilliant delineation of the men and actions in high circles in Tokyo that led to Japan's capitulation.

The China-Burma-India theater of the U.S. army was only a relatively small niche in the war in that region, though American leaders like Stilwell and Chennault loomed larger than life and had influence beyond their limited commands. Three titles stand above the rest on the Americans in the CBI: Charles F. Romanus and Riley Sunderland, *The China-Burma-India Theater,* 3 vols. (Washington, D.C., 1953–1959), comprehensive and fair; Charlton Ogburn, *The Marauders* (New York, 1959), a solid, lively account of the main American combat force in Burma; and Barbara W. Tuchman, *Stilwell and the American Experience in China, 1911–1945* (New York, 1971), a dramatically told and soundly researched account of Stilwell's long ties with China.

Five works on the home front convey well the complicated, dynamic relations between the military and the society and economy during the war years: John M. Blum, *V for Victory: Politics and American Culture During World War II* (New York, 1976), a masterful study of the main factors, especially cultural, that affected the nation and its war effort; William L. O'Neill, *A Democracy at War: America's Fight at Home and Abroad in World War II* (New York, 1993), the most recent contribution in this area and one of the most discerning; Allan M. Winkler, *Home Front USA: America During World War II* (Arlington Heights, Ill., 1986), insightful despite its brevity; Richard Polenberg, *War and Society: The United States, 1941–1945* (Philadelphia, 1972), noted for its fair and balanced approach; and Richard R. Lingeman, *Don't You Know There's a War On? The American Front, 1941–1945* (New York, 1970), a vivid, journalistic picture of the nation at war but filled with fresh research, especially on everyday life. David Brinkley, *Washington Goes to War* (New York, 1988), is an exciting, sometimes humorous "you-are-there" account of the hectic, always changing world of the national capital in wartime. Several good studies of African Americans encompass the war period, but the most relevant and useful on the wartime military experience is Ulysses Lee, *The Employment of Negro Troops* (Washington, D.C., 1966), a landmark study in the official army history series. Another noteworthy and pioneering work in that series is Mattie E. Treadwell, *The Women's Army Corps* (Washington, D.C., 1954), which, like Lee's fine effort, tries to communicate to readers a genuine sense of the opportunities, achievements, failures, and frustrations that women, as well as African Americans, encountered in the white-male-dominated American and civilian worlds of 1941–1945.

Index

A NOTE ON THE AUTHORS

D. Clayton James is the John Biggs Professor of Military History at Virginia Military Institute. Born in Winchester, Kentucky, he received a Ph.D. from the University of Texas and has held distinguished professorships at the Marine Corps Command and Staff College, Mississippi State University, the Army Command and General Staff College, and the Army War College. He has written widely on the history of the American armed forces, including eight books, the best known a three-volume biography, *The Years of MacArthur*.

Anne Sharp Wells, a native of Jackson, Mississippi, is a member of the administrative faculty of Virginia Military Institute. She holds graduate degrees from the University of Alabama and Mississippi State University. She has been president of the Society of Mississippi Archivists and editor of the *World War Two Studies Association Newsletter*, and has written two earlier books with D. Clayton James.